John Eliot Howard

The Quinology of the East Indian Plantations

John Eliot Howard

The Quinology of the East Indian Plantations

ISBN/EAN: 9783742826534

Manufactured in Europe, USA, Canada, Australia, Japa

Cover: Foto ©Thomas Meinert / pixelio.de

Manufactured and distributed by brebook publishing software
(www.brebook.com)

John Eliot Howard

The Quinology of the East Indian Plantations

THE

QUINOLOGY

OF THE

EAST INDIAN PLANTATIONS.

BY

JOHN ELIOT HOWARD, F.L.S., F.R.M.S., F.R.H.S.,

MEMBER OF THE PHARMACEUTICAL SOCIETY OF GREAT BRITAIN, AND OF THE BOTANICAL SOCIETY OF FRANCE; HONORARY
MEMBER OF THE NETHERLANDS INDUSTRIAL SOCIETY, AND OF THE PHYSICO-MEDICAL SOCIETY OF ERLANGEN.

LONDON:
L. REEVE & CO., 5, HENRIETTA STREET, COVENT GARDEN.
1869.

MICROSCOPICAL OBSERVATIONS.

It is important to observe that the whole of the sections in the first two Plates, and partially those in the third, are of the same species, *C. succirubra*, Pavon. It is evident on inspection that, whilst a certain family likeness prevails amongst those barks which have not been subjected to unnatural circumstances, there is yet some variation in the size and manner of dispersion of the fibres of the liber and of the laticiferous vessels; so that attempts to classify barks according to a too-precise system, resting specifically on such distinctions, would certainly end in confusion. In the renewed barks the characteristics are in part less distinct, so that the renewed barks of *C. succirubra* and of *C. officinalis* are seen to be much more like each other than they are to the species to which they respectively belong.

The external appearance of the specimens varies according to their place of growth. In Plate I. Fig. 1, the circumstance of being grown under dense shade gives the bark a suberous aspect, that of the *China rubra suberosa* of the Germans, which Dr. Berg derived from a separate species, the *C. coccinea* of Pavon.* It is well known to those who are familiar with the *C. succirubra* in its native forests, that the bark of the same tree will assume these different aspects, as it grows in a more or less exposed situation. The bark of Fig. 2 had more the aspect of the *Cortex China ruber durus* of Berg. That of Fig. 3 is remarkable for its poor appearance, and for the ease with which the external coat exfoliates.

The crystals of alkaloid are distinguished from those of raphides, which are found in the abnormal concretions, by their aspect and by the circumstance of their easy solubility in glycerine, in spirit, in water or in any menstruum which I know how to employ. They also polarize feebly, and present the appearance of different salts of quinine and other alkaloids present in the bark, which apparently the feeble alkaline ley has not at once been able to reach. The Fig. 1 section, remarkable for its abundance in cinchonine, is also remarkable (as I found in some thick sections) for an abundance of a peculiar concretion of crystalline masses in the region of the liber. These are not seen in Mr. West's figure, having been removed by the caustic. I presume that the crystals found in Fig. 2 and Fig. 3 belong to the salts of cinchonidine, though the *facies* of the crystals most resembles those of the alkaloid itself.

In Fig. 8 we find the appearance of a salt of quinine, and that chiefly in the cellular envelope. In Fig. 8 *a* the character of the crystals is more fully brought out, and contrasted with the earthy salts which fill some of the cells.

In Plate II. we are presented with the features of bark in varied stages of renewal. That in the early stage (Fig. 1) appears to be as yet very little organized, consisting almost entirely of ordinary cellular

---

* Berg's 'Anatomischer Atlas,' p. 64, note.

tissue, in which some few liber fibres are sparsely embedded, and also a number of abnormal concretions. A prolongation of a medullary ray seems to indicate the course of an active lateral circulation, and in the region of the liber may be seen a few small cells, of a shape that may indicate an approaching change to that structure which is seen in the region of the liber in the normal state, as in Plate I. Fig. 1, and also in the renewed bark in a state of greater advancement of organization in Fig. 2.

In this last bark (Fig. 2) we trace all the features of perfect organization, such as may be seen in bark in its natural state in Fig. 1. This may be compared with the remarks in the body of the volume (p. 19), but in Fig. 8, which is one stage further in the process of renewal, the bark having been *twice* stripped from the tree, this is much more evident, and I am really astonished at the perfectness and beauty of the organization. The bark was rich in quinine, and having probably been exposed to a warm temperature, although shielded by moss it also produced cinchonidine. The combined sulphates of these two alkaloids amounted to not less than 8·45 per cent.* against 5 per cent. from the first crop, represented in Fig. 2. The bark of Fig. 8 is consequently very rich in alkaloid, and " not only is the gross percentage of alkaloids larger than in the last decortication, but of this a more considerable percentage consists of quinine, and that less intimately combined with the yellow colouring-matter, so as to be more easily purified." The appearance of the Fig. 8 bark was decidedly more red in the bulk of the sample than that of Fig. 2 ; and this feature comes out so strongly in the microscopic sections, as drawn by Mr. West, that I have been induced to repeat sections of the bark recently, to satisfy myself whether this was an accidental feature or one which might be presumed common to the whole sample. It proved to be the latter ; the sections, even the thinnest, exhibiting the rounded cells filled with coloured contents, which characterize Fig. 8, Fig. 3, Fig. 7, of Plate II. I mention Fig. 8 first as the one which appears to be most fairly contrasted with Fig. 2 of the previous crop of renewed bark.

The growth must be rapid, since we are told by Mr. M'Ivor† that renewed bark of one season's growth is " quite as thick as ordinary bark of two or even three years' growth." I should connect with this fact the existence of the broad band of coloured cellular tissue extending from the liber to the suberous envelope. It seems to indicate a vigorous lateral circulation, and perhaps the conversion of some of the colouring-matters into resin, for this is favoured by the same circumstances of warm temperature, etc., which induce cinchonidine, of which there is a large amount in this bark. The structure of the bark (which I thought from my early examinations resembled the granulated flesh over a wound) is in this specimen (Fig. 8) singularly perfect, especially when the circumstances of its formation are taken into account ; and I think the bright colour must be owing to the early stage in which the nourishing sap, as derived from the wood, is found, in the full flow of sap and production of alkaloid ; when more fully oxidized, it dissolves easily in the caustic ley.

I found in my renewed experiments with this bark, crystals of some soluble salt of alkaloid, rather abundant in the cellular envelope, specially near the corky layer.

In Fig. 3 (from the same sample of bark) we have a less perfect, or rather a less normal organization, the structure between the liber and the suberous envelope being apparently disturbed by the intervention of the spiral and reticulate vessels.

Fig. 7 presents in longitudinal section the structure of the same bark in very ample detail. The suberous layer is very thin in this specimen, and the commencing change of the cellular tissue into cork is well marked ; also in the portion adjacent to the wood we may notice a rather unusual development of the liber-fibres, which occupy, nevertheless, but a small portion of the extent of the bark.

The whole of the sections of bark in Plate III., with the exception of Nos. 5 and 6, belong to the *C. succirubra*, and illustrate " the third crop of renewed bark " of which the analysis is given under E. in the

---

* 'Analysis of Fifth Remittance,' by J. E. Howard.   † 'Report' for 1864-5.

Appendix. The comparison with " the second crop of renewed bark " will there be found, and it will be seen that whilst there is a certain amount of increase in the total amount of the alkaloids obtained, yet in the production of crystallized sulphate of quinine there is a falling off in the third crop, and that it proved more difficult to work than the second.

The different season of the year at which the two crops of bark were gathered may have had something to do with this. The second crop was stripped from the trees in September and October, 1866, and, as it appears,[*] " at a season of full and luxuriant growth, when the sap is in full flow." It seems to me that the sections show the cellular structure to be gorged with recent supplies of nourishing sap, bringing with it abundance of the mother substance from the wood. This is probably just changing into Cinchona red and other products; among which the alkaloids are the most important, but the colouring matter the most manifest to the sight. At an early stage of oxidation this colouring matter is probably in a state comparable to that which I have described in another place.[†] A solution of pale liquor from red bark, after the fully oxidized Cinchona red had separated out by cooling, was mixed with isinglass, and when formed into a jelly, suffered to oxidize slowly; this it did very prettily, turning red from the outside ; ammonia greatly expedited the process. The colour in these sections partakes both of the Cinchona red tint and that of another colouring substance of the bark, which is probably simultaneously formed.

The bark from which the specimens in this present Plate III. was taken, was (on the other hand) gathered in March, which must be a period of complete rest to the plant ; for even in February, being the dry season, this is said to be the case,[‡] and " the sap begins to rise in the early part of April." Everything in the appearance of the specimens seems to agree well with the period of rest. The abundance of liber fibres well filled up even to the region of the cambium—the segregation of the different products of vegetation into different regions of the bark, all coincide well with this view.

Resin is *deposited* in abundance near the outside, and some other indications in the same zone direct attention to the deteriorating change which goes forward in the outer bark, even to some extent when this is mossed.

In the liber are seen feathery crystals as of a kinovate, and, in the lax cellular tissue, globular concretions of imperfect crystalline structure (some also transparent and homogeneous) of more soluble salts of quinine; such I judge these to be from finding this state of things common in rich Calisaya bark. The lax fibre of the cellular envelope in the Calisaya is often filled with such masses, sometimes reminding of the appearance of candied honey.

I cannot help connecting with the above state of things the large proportion of uncrystallizable quinine in this third crop. My own view of the matter (differing from some able chemists, and which therefore, though sustained by experiments of my own, I express with reserve) is that this amorphous condition of quinine is not one connected with its *formation*, but with its *degradation*, and this latter in some way through the influence of resin which is associated with it at the same time. The same circumstances, viz. heat and light, which favour the production of cinchonidine, are noticed by both Mr. Broughton and myself to favour that of resin ; and as these must tell most on the outside of the bark, we have a reason for that deposition of resin near the cork, which is evident in many of the sections. It is particularly difficult to purify cinchonidine from resin.

More extended researches will indicate the proper season for gathering the bark ; but the conclusions to be drawn from the examination of the *second* and *third* crop of renewed bark seem, as far as they go, to indicate the period of the full flow of the sap as more favourable than that of the repose of the plant for obtaining the maximum of quinine in a crystallizable state.

---

* W. G. M'Ivor to Sec. Gov., 3rd Oct. 1863, No. 91 also.   † Illustr. Nueva Quinologia, Mic. Illustr. p. 8.
‡ W. G. M'Ivor to Sec. Gov., 17 March, 1864; also 3rd May, 1865.

Mr. West noted the section (Fig. 1) as most interesting to him.   The small size and lax character of the cellular tissues, the different conditions of the alkaloid salts in different portions of the bark, and the numerous prolongations of medullary rays in very pale tissue particularly arrested his attention ; but there is more even than appears at first sight, for by comparison with Fig. 6 of this same Plate it will be seen that, as to the size and shape of the cells, both these barks have put on the same appearance, which also corresponds in part to that of the richest Calisaya barks,* though not entirely confined to these.   It is not so evident why this should so be, as it is that this lax cell-structure is favourable to the production of quinine.

Fig. 2 shows this structure still more clearly, together with the included alkaloids.

Fig. 3 brings out the characteristic features of these rounded aggregations of crystalline matter from the same, drawn with the camera *in situ*, but without the cells.

Fig. 4 shows the whole section of bark under small magnifying power, giving the whole detail of structure, both of the old and new bark and their junction, which must be understood to be about *x*, the part to the left of which is renewed, whilst the portion to the right retains its normal appearance.

Fig. 5 and Fig. 6 represent different ends of one and the same quill about 10 inches long sent to me by Mr. M'Ivor in the eighth remittance which I have previously described.   About 2 inches of one end are labelled " *Chinchona crispa*, original bark under moss, 5 years old, 1868."   About 6 inches more remaining of the renewed end are labelled " *Chinchona crispa*, renewed bark under moss 1 year old."   This though as thick, or even thicker than the unrenewed part, is distinguishable at first sight from the latter, and the point of junction is quite evident. The unrenewed part has the appearance of the " *Colorada del Rey* " bark, but I have simply described it as *C. officinalis*, without defining the variety.   The remarkable point in the microscopic section is the entire contrast in structure between the two ends of the *same* quill, a contrast which would surely cause these to rank as different species, if judged according to the rules laid down in the Anatomical Atlas of Dr. Berg ; I am not able to say whether an equal contrast prevails in the richness of the alkaloidal contents.   The zone of liber fibres in Fig. 6 is very remarkable, as also the numerous and prolonged medullary rays, extending to the corky layer, and probably telling of rapid growth.

Fig. 7 shows a section of the third crop of renewed bark under the curiously disturbing influence of the spiral tissue, which is seen in isolated portions as well as in bunches ; the pale colour of the adjacent portions is well represented, having the appearance of being subjected to the exhaustion of contents by the proximity of this spiral tissue.   One spiral will be seen running a little within the corky layer and parallel to it, for a considerable distance.   Towards the upper part of the figure we have lines of cells, and incipient medullary rays placed directly at right angles to those on which they abut.

Fig. 8. With regard to the actual fact of different forms of spiral being present in the same section, this has been well noted by Henfrey in the ' Micrographic Dictionary,' under the heading " Spiral Structures," but it is not less interesting to add to the number of examples in which the fact has been recognized and carefully represented.

---

* Berg's ' Anatomischer Atlas,' Taf. xxx.; Weddell, Histoire, tab. 1, f. 27, et alia inedita.

SECTIONS OF BARK.

PLATE I.

Fig. 1. *C. succirubra*, from Ceylon, *grown in the forest under dense shade.*—*a*, the suberous coat; *b*, cells becoming changed into cork; *c*, prolongation of the medullary rays; *d*, laticiferous vessels; *f*, liber-fibre, cut transversely; *g*, fibre not yet filled up with layers of incrusting-matter; *h*, indications of the cambium layer. × 50 diameters.

Fig. 2. *C. succirubra*, from Ceylon, *grown in open garden.*—*a*, the suberous coat; *b*, cells compressed and undergoing change; *c*, the prolonged medullary rays opening out into cellular tissue of ordinary structure; *d*, laticiferous vessels; *e*, cellular tissue of the liber in smaller polygonal, or globular cells; *f*, fibres of the liber; *h*, point of junction with the wood, forming a cinnamon-coloured inner surface of the dried bark; *i*, crystals of alkaloid. × 100 diameters.

Fig. 2 *a*. Portions of cellular tissue of the above, showing more distinctly the crystals above mentioned; *i*, crystals, probably of cinchonidine; *j*, small globular aggregations, probably of alkaloid, united with cerotic acid. × 100 diameters.

Fig. 2 *b*. The same crystals as above. × 200 diameters.

Fig. 5. *C. succirubra*, from Ceylon, *grown in the open garden, six feet apart.*—*a*, the suberous, *d*, the laticiferous vessels; *e*, liber-fibres of larger dimension; *h*, dark brown inner surface; *i*, crystals of alkaloid. × 50 diameters.

Fig. 5 *a*. Portion of cellular tissue of the above; *i*, crystals, probably of cinchonidine; *j*, globular concretions; *k*, isolated crystal; *l*, abnormal formation, a cell filled with granulations of some earthy compound (insoluble in any menstruum employed), also colouring-matter. × 100 diameters.

Fig. 5 *b*. Groups of the above crystals, and also isolated crystals. × 200 diameters.

Fig. 8. *C. succirubra*, original bark, six months under moss.—*a*, the suberous coat; *i*, crystals, probably of kinovate of quinine; *l*, abnormal concretions; *d*, laticiferous vessel; *f*, fibres of the liber; *e*, lax cellular tissue; *h*, internal surface, with indications of the cambium. × 50 diameters.

Fig. 8 *a.*—*i*, groups of crystals, as above; *l*, abnormal concretion. × 100 diameters.

PLATE II.

Fig. 1. *C. succirubra*, bark in *an early stage of renewal*, from Ootacamund.—*a*, the suberous coat; *c*, cellular tissue, which apparently marks the course of the circulation from the medullary rays to the external coat; *f*, isolated liber-fibre (two seen in juxtaposition on the reverse side); *l*, abnormal concretions; *c*, lax cellular structure (favourable to the production of quinine); *h*, indication of cambium. × 50 diameters.

Fig. 2. *C. succirubra*, *first crop of renewed bark*, from Ootacamund.—*a*, thick, suberous coat; *b*, layer of cells, filled with resinous deposit; *m*, cellular envelope of cell-structure, resembling specimen (Plate II. Fig. 2, 'Quinologia '); *d*, large laticiferous duct; *c*, cells of normal structure, forming continuation of the parenchyma of the medullary rays; *e*, liber-fibres, normal in character and position; *g*, young liber-fibres not filled up; *h*, hard inner surface. × 50 diameters.

Fig. 3. *C. succirubra*, *second crop of renewed bark.*—*a*, the suberous coat; *b*, cellular structure, apparently gorged with resin, changing into cork; *n*, spiral or reticulate vessels; *m*, normal structure of the cellular envelope; *e*, lax cellular structure, in places filled with cincho-tannic acid in an early stage of oxidation; *c*, course of the prolongation of a medullary ray; *f*, normal liber-fibres; *h*, hard and coloured inner bark. × 50 diameters.

Fig. 4. Spiral and reticulate vessels from the above at *n*, simply spiral vessels. × 100 diameters.

Fig. 5. Spiral and reticulate vessels (from a transverse section of the above Fig. 3); *m*, the cellular tissue coloured by resin; *n*, the ends of reticulate vessels; *o*, vessels of the cellular tissue, apparently emptied of their colouring-matters by contact with the spiral vessels. × 100 diameters.

Fig. 6. Natural size of section, at *n* showing the position of the spiral vessels.

Fig. 7. *C. succirubra*, *second crop of renewed bark (long. sect.)*—*a*, the suberous layer; *m*, cellular tissue; *d*, the same, surrounding laticiferous duct; *e*, cells of parenchyma, gorged with colouring-matter; *f*, fibres of the liber. × 50 diameters.

Fig. 8. *C. succirubra*, *second crop of renewed bark* (probably exposed to greater heat).—*a*, the suberous coat; *b*, current of colouring and probably resinous matter from the medullary rays to the bark; *c*, lax cellular tissue; *i*, crystals of alkaloid; *d*, laticiferous ducts; *e*, globular cells of parenchyma, filled with colouring-matter; *l*, abnormal concretions; *f*, fibres of the liber; *h*, internal surface, with trace of cambium. × 50 diameters.

Fig. 8 *a*. Crystals of alkaloid, seen in the parenchyma of the above. × 100 diameters.

Fig. 10. Fibres of the liber, probably from *C. Palton* (see p. 23). × 50 diameters.

c

PLATE III.

Fig. 1. *Third crop of renewed bark of C. succirubra.*— *a*, the suberous layer; *b*, deposit of resin in the cellular tissue about to change into cork; *m*, abnormal concretions; *i* and *j*, abundant deposit of soluble salts of quinine; *c*, prolongation of medullary ray; *k*, crystals of a kinovate; *f*, liber-fibres; *n*, inner surface with trace of cambium.   × 50 diameters.

Fig. 2. Lax cellular tissue from the above, full of alkaloid.   × 100 diameters.

Fig. 3. Globular concretion of the above alkaloids without cellular tissue; *j*, crystalline masses; *i*, transparent globes.   × 200 diameters.

Fig. 4. *Third crop of renewed bark*, and its junction with the old bark, drawing of complete section; *a*, suberous coat; *m*, medullary rays contorted; *f*, sharp line of demarcation between liber and cellular tissue; *h*, liber-fibres; *x*, abnormal formation, probably marking the division between the old and the new bark.   × 10 diameters.

Fig. 5. *Unrenewed end of C. officinalis quill*, 5 years old; *a*, the suberous layer; *b*, changing into cork; *m*, ordinary cellular tissue; *f*, liber-fibre; *j*, prolonged medullary ray; *h*, traces of the cambium.   × 50 diameters.

Fig. 6. *Renewed end of quill of C. officinalis*, nearly a year and a half old; *a*, the suberous layer; *b*, deposit of resin in cellular tissue changing into cork; *c*, lax cellular tissue; *i* and *j*, the same full of alkaloid; *f*, congeries of liber-fibres; *c*, prolonged medullary ray; *h*, remains of cambium layer.   × 50 diameters.

Fig. 7. *Renewed bark of third crop*, with spiral tissue; *a*, the suberous layer; *b*, pale cellular tissue; *n*, spiral tissue longitudinally placed; *o*, bunches of spiral tissue.   × 20 diameters.

Fig. 8. Portions of spirals from the above bark; *a*, partially unwound, showing the angularity of the fibre; *b*, annuli; *c*, scalariform-like tissue; *d*, joined as spirals usually do; *e*, portion somewhat netted, and with the abrupt junction characteristic of reticular tissue.   × 350 diameters.

PLATE I.

Fig: 1.

× 50.

Fig: 2ᵃ.

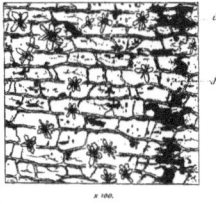

× 100.

Fig: 2.

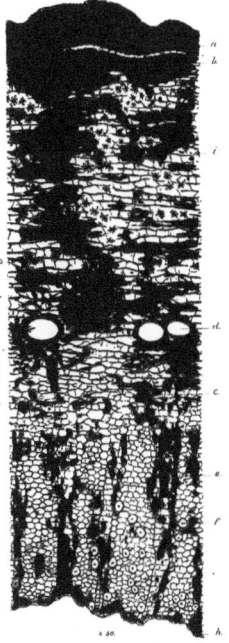

Fig: 2ᵇ.

× 200.

Fig: 5ᵃ.

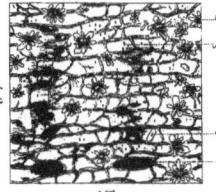

× 100.

Alkaloid.

Grown in the open garden.

Fig: 5.

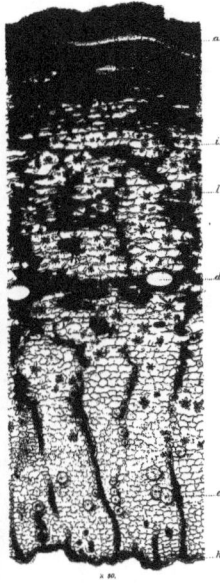

× 50.

Fig: 5ᵇ.

× 200.

Fig: 8ᵃ.

× 100.

Crystals of

Fig: 8.

Six months under moss.

× 50.

PLATE 17

Fig. 3.

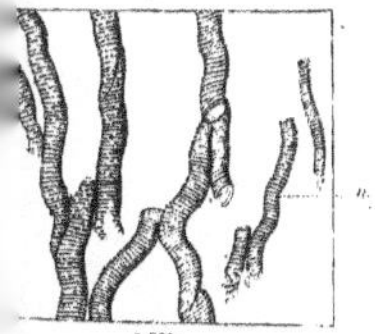

Fig. 1.

Bark in an early stage of renewal.

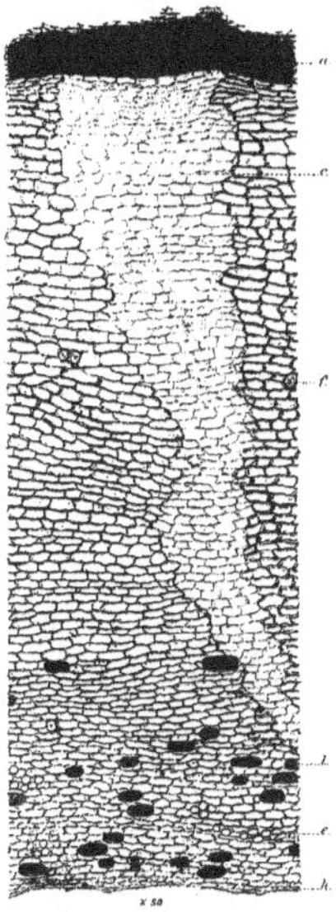

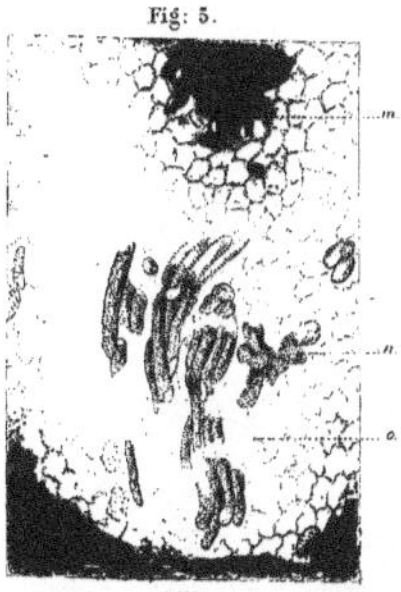

Fig. 2.

First crop of renewed bark.

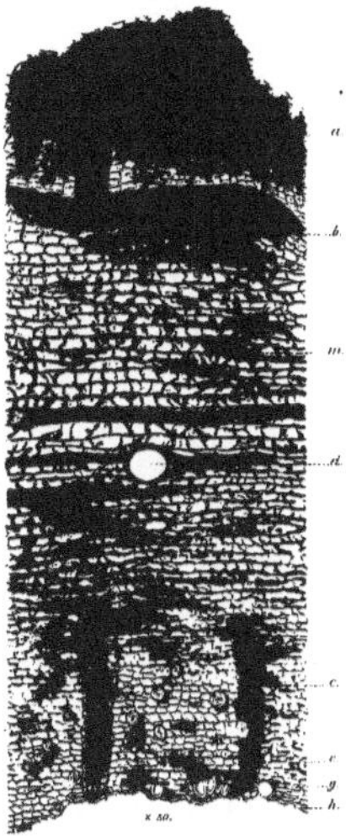

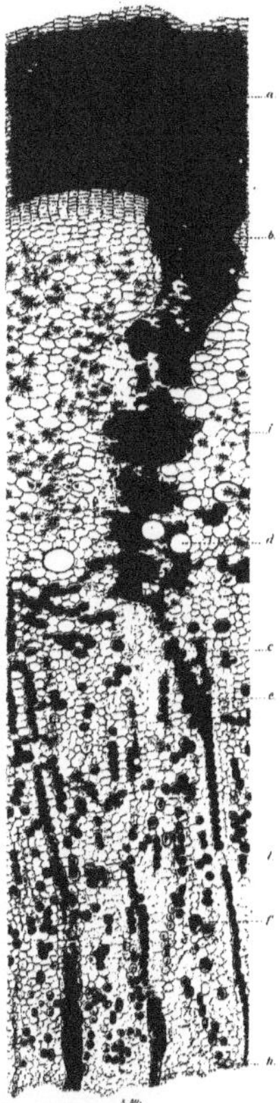

Fig. 7.

Second crop of renewed bark (long. sect.)

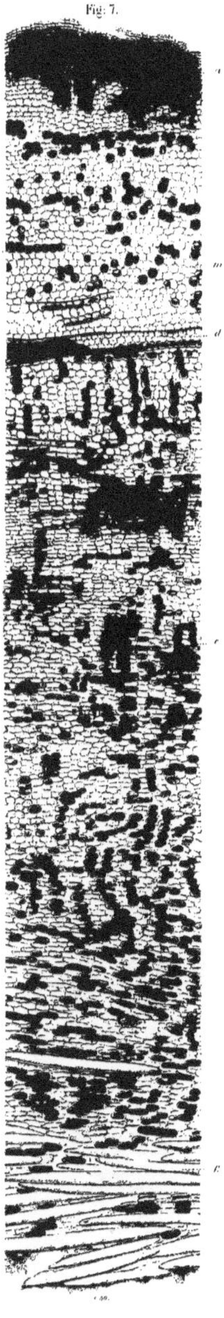

Fig. 10.

Fibres of the liber.

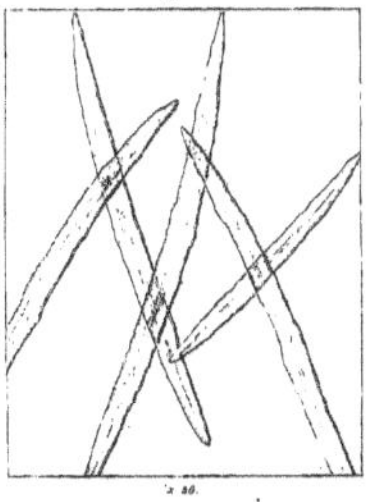

Fig. 6.

Spiral vessels.

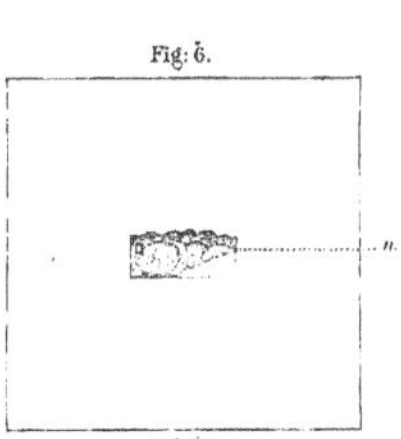

Fig. 8.

Second crop of renewed bark.

Fig. 5.

Spiral or reticulate vessels.

Fig. 4.

Fig. 5.a

Crystals of albumeid.

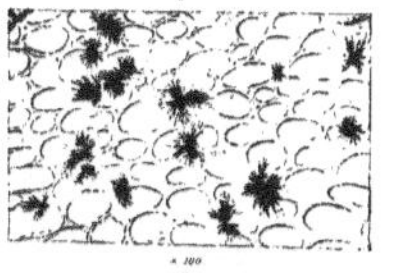

PLATE II

Fig: 1.

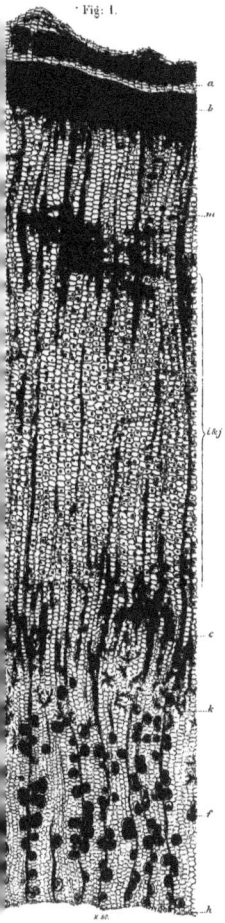

Fig: 2.

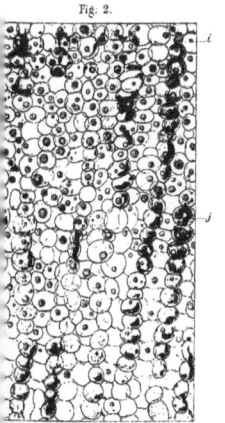

Fig: 5.

Outward end of C. officinalis quill. (5 years old.)

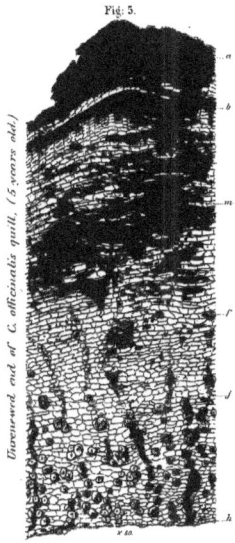

Fig: 3.

Globular concretions.

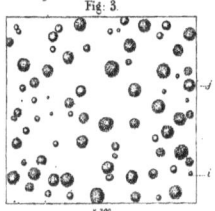

Fig: 4.

Third crop of renewed bark & its junction with the old bark.
drawing of complete section.

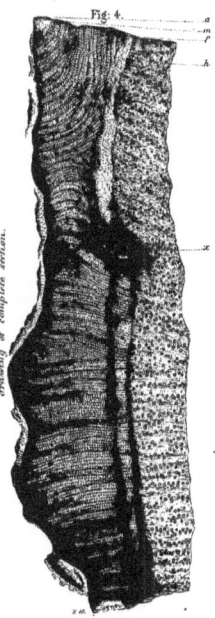

Fig: 6.

Renewed end of quill of C. officinalis.

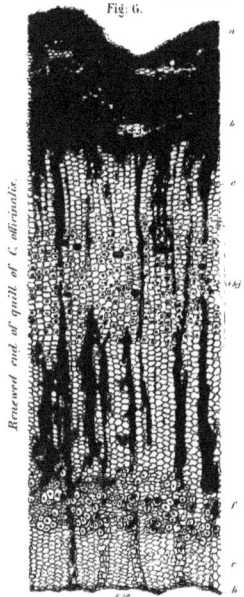

Fig: 8.

Portions of spirals from cinchona bark.

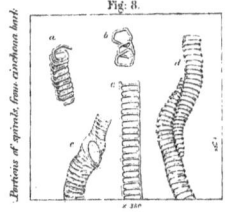

Fig: 7.

Spiral tissue in renewed bark. (of the third crop)

QUINOLOGY

EAST INDIAN PLANTATIONS.

PART I.

CHEMICAL AND MICROSCOPICAL INVESTIGATIONS.

Introductory Remarks.

THE chemical and microscopical investigations contained in the present Part are strictly in continuation of the kindred researches in my previous works, and, although by no means complete or exhaustive, may afford some practical assistance in the great and beneficent undertaking of the naturalization of the Quinine-producing trees in India.

I defer for the present any detailed remarks on the botanical aspects of the varied species of Cinchona* now under cultivation, the more especially as I am informed by J. Broughton, Esq., the Quinologist appointed by Government to the chemical oversight of the plantations at Ootacamund, that he has instituted and is carrying forward varied observations on the influence of soil and climate, and especially of elevation above the sea-level, on these plants, the results of which will doubtless present many novel and most important facts confirmatory or otherwise of views here advanced by me. The Indian Government has been fortunate in the choice of servants to whom the practical carrying out of the details of this great scheme has been confided, and I am glad to think that in this most recent instance they have been equally successful. It is not for me to award the meed of praise to those whose toils and dangers in the service entitle them to the gratitude of the world; but it may be permitted me, as having previously given what assistance I could render in the analysis of the specimens sent home from various parts of India, to bear my unbiassed testimony to Mr. Broughton's skill and diligence, as evidenced by what he has already accomplished in a peculiarly difficult line of chemical investigation.

Elevation above the Sea-Level.

Recent observations on this point may save the apparently useless attempt to cultivate these plants at a level below 4000 feet above the ocean; I refer for the full elucidation of the subject to the results of Mr. Broughton's observations, which I hope to see published.

---

* I adhere to the old Linnean term, but quote from my correspondents as I find the word spelt by them.

B

Mr. M'Ivor remarks that the Red Bark tree especially has found, in its new home in plantations on the Neilgherries, "conditions quite as favourable to its growth and full development as in the most favourable localities in the Andes."

"The *C. succirubra, Peruviana,* and *micrantha* thrive on the Nedivuttum and Pykara plantations at elevations varying from 4000 to 6000 feet; while *C. officinalis, Bonplandiana,* and *crespilla* continue to grow more sturdy and vigorous on the Dodabetta plantations at elevations varying from 7000 to 8500 feet. These latter species grow equally well upon grass as upon forest land, and bear almost every exposure, hence they can be successfully cultivated over the whole plateau of the Neilgherries, excepting such land-locked hollows as are subject to severe frosts."[*]

"A few plants of the *Calisaya* accidentally planted out at a high elevation, 7300 feet, seem to have adopted a much more luxuriant habit than those planted at lower elevations. Several plants of the *C. Calisaya* planted in the first Denison plantation in November, 1862, are now (1865) in full bloom, presenting a most beautiful appearance, while their fragrance fills the air for a considerable distance."

Mr. Broughton informs me that the *C. succirubra,* above 7500 feet, yields little more than two per cent. of alkaloid, and that destitute of Quinine and Quinidine, and that below 5000 feet the bark is thinner (which agrees with specimens sent me from the Wynaad and other places). Mr. Broughton adds, "that it appears to contain Quinidine in larger amount, and a large quantity of the vexatious resin," about which I had written to him. "In the Crown Barks the highest elevations yield bark of about even quantity down to 6500 feet. Below this the amount of alkaloid becomes somewhat less, and instead of Quinine, Chinchonidine and Quinidine are met with. At low elevations the trees do not thrive, and the resin of the bark becomes as troublesome as in the Red Bark."

It will be thus evident that the Crown Barks are adapted to the higher elevation, and the Red Bark to a lower. This might have been anticipated from what we know of their growth in their native habitat. The large leaves of the *C. succirubra* are liable to injury from strong winds, and the plant suffers in consequence; but I am informed, by one of the cultivators in Ceylon, that at the higher altitudes the plant shows considerable power of adaptation to the climate, and the leaves assume a somewhat different appearance.

Of all the varieties of Crown Barks, the *C. officinalis,* var. *crispa,*[†] has long been esteemed the most hardy; and I may here record the additional observation that this sort succeeded well with me in the open air last summer, and though I had to remove it to shelter under glass in November,[‡] it did not then need more warmth than the half-hardy exotics. It seems to me that its requirements are so little in excess of those of the common *Arbutus* (which does not stand the winter with me), that where this flourishes in a mild and equable and moist climate, as at Killarney,[§] I believe this *crespilla* sort might possibly be naturalized, although I am far from supposing it could there be grown to profit commercially, as the growth would be much too slow to admit of this. In other respects it appears, by Mr. Broughton's examination, to be a good variety. My own investigation gave me, from bark carefully mossed by Mr. M'Ivor when three years and a half old, the following product:—

Sulphate of Quinine	. .	2·46
Uncrystallized ditto	. .	·44
		—— 2·90
Cinchonicine .	.	·86
Total .	.	3·76

* See Return, East India Cinchona Plant, ordered by the House of Commons to be printed, June 18, 1866, 353, p. 162.
† "The tree of the *crespilla* is the same with that of the *amarilla* and *colorada,* but grows in a cold, frosty climate."—*Arrot, in a Paper communicated to the Royal Society in* 1737.
"No. 2, *crespilla,* found growing, in general, in a deposit of peat on the summit of the highest mountains around Loja, where the temperature sometimes falls to 27° Fahr."—*R. Cross,* 1861.
‡ Again planted out in the open ground in April, 1868, but needing protection from severe spring frosts.
§ "Mean summer temperature, 59¼° Fahr., mean winter temperature, 44¼°. *Laurus nobilis* attains to a height of upwards of 30 feet."—*Dr. Moore, Rep. Bot. Congress,* 1866, *p.* 173.

The Quinine was associated with some Cinchonidine. My previous experiments were less satisfactory, perhaps owing to the great abundance of green colouring-matter found in this bark ; and perhaps, also, as regards the specimens from Loja, owing to the very immature state in which they were gathered.

Change of Place of Growth as affecting Successive Generations of C. officinalis.

Any addition to the amount of our knowledge on the effects of change of climate on these plants must be valuable to the cultivator, and I have no doubt that those so engaged will read with interest the following examination of three generations of one species, the *C. officinalis* of Linnæus, growing respectively in South America, England (under glass), and in India.

The original bark of the first generation, from the mountains of Uritusinga, near Loja (Peru), was sent to me, with the flowering branches and ripened seeds, by Don T. Riofrio, and from these I raised plants in 1859. This was fine-looking, but very much weathered Crown Bark, with few adherent lichens, it gave me :—

No. 1.

FIRST GENERATION.

Oxalate of Quinine .	. . .	1·87
Cinchonidine .	. . .	1·20
Cinchonine .	.	·04
	Total . .	3·11

No. 2.

SECOND GENERATION RAISED FROM THE ABOVE SEED.

No. 2 *a.*	No. 2 *b.*
Grown in England.	*Grown partly in England, partly in India.*
Sulphate of Quinine . . . . 1·36	Oxalate of Quinine . . . . 1·40
Cinchonicine (with merely a trace of	Quinine uncrystallized . ·17 = 1·57
Cinchonine) . . . . ·57	Cinchonicine . . . ·79
Total . 1·93	Total . . 2·36

No. 3.

THIRD GENERATION, DESCENDED FROM No. 2 *b.*

Sulphate of Quinine	. .	1·75
Sulphate of Cinchonidine	. .	1·50
Cinchonine . ..	. .	·08
	Total .	3·33

In the third generation[*] it is easy to remark a sort of *atavism*, the produce having returned almost exactly to the first; and having, in the Neilgherries, in India, rather surpassed the quantity of alkaloid yielded by the first generation grown on the mountains of Uritusinga, its native habitat.

This is so far very satisfactory, as showing that at least there is no deterioration in this species through the so great change of its acclimatization; and I am strongly of opinion that experience will manifest a still further decided improvement, especially consequent upon the effects of *mossing* the bark.[†]

---

[*] The analysis of this No. 3 I owe to Mr. Broughton.
[†] A specimen from Mr. Thwaites, apparently of this sort, grown in Ceylon, gave me :—

Sulphate of Quinine .	3·93	
Quinine uncrystallized .	2·41	
		6·34
Cinchonidine . .		·51
Cinchonine . .		·28
	Total . .	7·18

I must direct particular attention to the fact that the variation of soil, temperature, and elevation united (all these being of the greatest extent) did not equal the effects of the altered character of *light* on the plant,—at least if I read the indications aright.

The first and third generations had probably an equal exposure to the sunlight and to the weather; but the second generation, raised under glass* (with enfeebled actinic power in the light, and in winter a greatly diminished, and in summer an excessive amount of this stimulus), shows a loss of product of alkaloid to the extent of more than one-third, and a still further deterioration in the substitution of Cinchonicine for the far more useful product Cinchonidine. The loss of product in Quinine is smaller in proportion, for reasons that will presently be noticed.

The plant sent to India (2 *b*) recovered only partially its tone of production. It was about six feet in height when I presented it to the Government, and it was then quite a flourishing young tree, but in its passage from Madras to the mountains suffered by a sunstroke, and lost all its leaves. It was with difficulty recovered; but by the skill of Mr. M'Ivor was so entirely restored that it yielded many thousand young plants, and these are so constantly multiplying, that this gentleman intends to plant sixty acres with these alone.

The bark of this (2 *b*) plant was sent home to me last summer by the Indian authorities for analysis, and yielded as above.

Effect of Sunlight.

I have before remarked a particular sensitiveness to the action of sunlight in the Cinchonæ, especially in some of the more delicately-formed species; and I now present my examination† of the bark of *C. succirubra*, sent home by Mr. Thwaites from Ceylon, showing the different effect of growth in deep shade, in more partial, and in full sunlight. I thought this well-devised experiment worthy to be followed up by the most complete examination, microscopical as well as chemical, in my power. The chemical examination, as reported to the Government, is as under:

No. 1. Bark of *C. succirubra*, taken from trees grown in the forest *under dense shade*. Plants planted out 8th February 1862, yields (1866) :—

Sulphate of Quinine	1·48
Cinchonidine	·61
Cinchonine	2·54
Total	4·63

The proportion of Cinchonine (including Cinchonicine) in this sample is very remarkable.

No. 2. Bark of *C. succirubra* taken from trees growing in the open garden, planted twenty-five feet apart, on the same day as the last.

Sulphate of Quinine	2·35	
Quinine uncrystallized	·95	
		3·30
Cinchonidine	1·11	
Cinchonine	·58	
Total		4·99

---

* This plant (No. 2 *a*), which I was obliged to cut down (January, 1866) has again (May, 1868) grown up to above seven feet in height, and is more vigorous than before.

† Return, etc., p. 379.

In this specimen, grown in full sunlight, the Quinine and Cinchonidine may be looked upon as more than doubled, and the Cinchonine reduced by three-quarters.

No. 3. Bark of *C. succirubra*, taken from trees planted in the open garden six feet apart, on June 1, 1863.

Sulphate of Quinine .		.	1·90
Quinine, uncrystallized	. .	1·18	3·08
Cinchonidine	.	.	·53
Cinchonine	.	.	·32
	Total .	.	3·93

The Cinchonidine is diminished one-half, and the Cinchonine in almost the same proportion, the Quinine has suffered less. The time of planting-out I suspect to have been less favourable in this case.

Microscopical Observations on the above Specimens.

No. 1, grown in the forest under dense shade, presents a very regular and beautiful microscopical structure, which, however, did not indicate superiority in produce of Quinine. I observed no crystallized alkaloid in this section.

No. 2, grown in full sunshine, has also a regular and promising structure. The laticiferous vessels are rather large. The crystals of alkaloid, probably of some salt of Cinchonidine, become conspicuous in this section.

No. 3, planted out sixteen months later, and in the month of June, has a comparatively shrivelled and unhealthy look, such as I have described in reference to the section of *C. Pahudiana* grown in Java;[*] the same abnormal formations also occur; so that I am not inclined to draw any absolute deductions from the chemical analysis of this peculiar specimen. I am satisfied that there have been some unfavourable conditions existing either in the season of planting or in the manner in which this was done.

The general result of these experiments[†] is, that sunlight favours the production of Cinchonidine and dense shade that of Cinchonine, whilst it appears from other observations that the most favourable circumstances for Quinine are, that the leaves should be well exposed to light whilst the stem-bark is shaded from the direct action of the sun.

Success of the Acclimatization of the Cinchonæ in India.

In reference to this question, I must refer the reader to some extracts from the very able and impartial address of Dr. Weddell to the Botanical Congress held in 1867, in Paris, which will be found in the Appendix.

My own belief is, that success, though not to the fullest possible extent, has been assured by the steps already taken; but it would not be well to overlook the fact that in Java[‡] some disappointment has

---

[*] See Illustr. Nueva Quin. plate iii. fig. 34, Micr. Secs.

[†] I am glad to find that in one point these observations coincide with remarks made by Mr. Broughton, who says in a letter to me (under date July 28, 1867) :—" Some Crown Barks grown under partial shade, which I examined, yielded but little Cinchonidine, whereas those in full sunshine yielded one and a half per cent. I believe you will find little in the plants in your conservatory, and should be greatly interested to know the results should you ever analyse their bark." (Vide No. 2, p. 3.)

[‡] A Report by Van Gorkom, which has just reached me, speaks, however, very hopefully, especially of the prospects of the *Calisaya* plants, of which three or four varieties are growing in Java. It is specially remarked that about 3000 plants raised from seed from British India, present a quite peculiar character, which partly belongs to the *C. micrantha*. I assisted at the purchase of the bag of seeds (collected by Lechler) for British India, to which no doubt this refers, and having some growing freely, side by side with the *C. micrantha*, brought by Pritchard from Huanuco, can quite confirm this resemblance. The plants are, I think, those of the *C. micrantha (Bolivian variety)*, of Weddell.

The plantations in Java have, by the last accounts (fourth quarter of 1867) suffered somewhat from heavy rains. The number of plants is as follows :—497·320 *C. Calisaya* ; 5·559 *C. succirubra* ; 18·569 *C. Condaminea* ; 0·559 *C. lancifolia* ; 0·385 *C. micrantha*. It is said that "a recent chemical examination of young roots of the *C. Pahudiana* appears to allow that this sort should attract new attention in order to be further cultivated." They appear to have been examined by Maier, with "not unfavourable" results, but the Report of Van Gorkom wishes to say little till more is known.—*Flora*, 1867, 1868, *Regensburg*.

C

been felt, and it is only by avoiding errors in the choice of species, and by carefully selecting the best situations and modes of culture, that individual planters in other parts of the world will see their efforts crowned with remunerative results.

It was at first a somewhat doubtful and anxious inquiry whether the product in alkaloids might not be deteriorated or altered by the change of climate to which these plants were to be subjected. It was with no small satisfaction, therefore, that in June, 1863, I first succeeded in obtaining from bark of the second year's growth in India the same alkaloids, and in equal quantity, as from bark grown in South America. Since then, it has been shown that the Cinchona, when cultivated, not only yield their normal proportion of alkaloid, but that, in some species at least, this is susceptible of a large increase.*

First Importations from India.

Another stage has now been reached, since the first importation of Quinine-producing bark from the East Indies, as a commercial article, took place in August of 1867. This first consignment was the product of six hundred small trees of *C. succirubra* (Red Bark), grown at Ootacamund, and on the Denison estate, and cut down and sent into the market by way of experiment. It was all contained in three large chests; thus showing that the plantation was far too young to afford, when thus treated, any adequate return to the cultivators. Moreover the chests, numbered respectively 1, 2, and 3, were by no means of equal value; although it so happened, that when exposed to public sale they brought nearly the same price per pound,— a circumstance tending to mislead the grower. The contents of No. 1 consisted in the bark of the stem; No. 2, of the large branches; and No. 3, of the small twigs; and these last were so poor in the yield of alkaloid that, when added to No. 2, the whole produce of the latter two chests would not have more than equalled that of the No. 1, containing the fine stem-bark. This was really fine, although the proper red colour of the bark itself was not yet developed. It consisted in pieces sometimes two feet in length, doubly curled inwards upon themselves, being not more than one-sixteenth of an inch in thickness. The diameter of the trees, for the time of growth, must have been large. The external appearance was long-wrinkled, with some slight cross cracks and protuberances, and in places traces of commencing lichens. Dr. De Vry informs me that No. 1 of *C. succirubra*, from Sir W. Denison's plantation, gave him 6·8 alkaloids, containing 2·85 Quinine. The rest was Cinchonidine, with a small quantity of Cinchonine. One of his former pupils obtained from this bark, by repeated decoctions with water, thirty-eight per cent. of extract, whilst American bark very seldom produces more than twenty-five per cent.

This first importation was attended with a curious result, which, having some possible bearing on the future, it may be well here to notice. It appeared that the bark, when submitted as usual to the examination and chemical analysis of those proposing to become purchasers, was differently estimated in England, France, and Germany. In England and France the variation of estimate does not demand notice,—depending in part on the mode in which the averages were taken; but in Germany a different result followed,—the agent for one manufacturer declaring that it contained no Quinine, but altogether another substance. I have shown that this species is particularly difficult to analyse; and it is quite probable that this chemist obtained all the product as Kinovate of Quinine, which would account for the statement. At all events it is important to let this incorrectness be known, since otherwise the notion may be propagated again so as to disquiet the minds of the cultivators. This effect, however, might not be injurious, if it operated as a check to over-production, which the map of the district published by Mr. Markham suggests (from the number of the plantations) as the chief danger to be now dreaded.†

Nothing can be more satisfactory than the luxuriance of the young trees in some situations. This is

---

* See in Appendix, First Report on the Bark and Leaves of *C. succirubra* grown in India, by J. E. H., to the Under-Secretary of State for India.

† Attempts at culture of the Cinchona have also been made, with more or less success, in Jamaica, in the Island of La

well shown in a photograph which Colonel Scott has recently had the goodness to send me of a portion of his plantation.* The characteristic features of the *C. succirubra* and the *C. nitida* are very manifest in this Plate.

The first instalment of the produce of the plantations in Ceylon, consisting of two small chests, has recently (April, 1868) been sold by public auction in London. The bark was that of *C. succirubra* and of *C. officinalis*, of only three years' growth, and consequently very immature. The bark of the *C. officinalis* was ascertained to contain already a good proportion of Quinine, having found a climate suited to its development.

The price per pound which was commanded in the open market for home consumption was higher than that of South American bark of the same age and species, since it proved to be superior in yield of alkaloid to that derived from the tree in its native habitat. Cultivation, in fact, had produced its usual effect, by removing as far as possible injurious agencies and surrounding the plant with circumstances qualified to secure its growth and vigour.

This is the favourable side of the question; but it must be admitted that the increase is slow, although fostered by the genial climate of the mountains of India, and that cultivators must make up their minds to wait longer than is convenient for returns from their outlay of capital, unless the production of bark can be in some manner accelerated.

Mossing the Bark.

Under these circumstances, it is well that Mr. M'Ivor should have discovered the plan of renewing the bark, after it has been removed from portions of the tree, by the simple application of moss, kept continually moist, thus allowing the plant time and favourable opportunity to repair the damage done to its structure. This damage would otherwise be fatal to the whole scheme, and hence the old writers exclaim against the injury thus inflicted upon the trees at Loja,† where the experiment of partial decortication was first tried. I received from Mr. M'Ivor, in 1864, a section of a tree which has been thus treated in India, and which most conclusively shows the great amount of injury it had received. Not only is the woody portion less developed than would normally have been the case, where the bark has been removed on the two opposite sides, but the wood itself is also partially deprived of its vitality and tending towards decay.

Mr. M'Ivor tells us that his "idea of artificially applying moss to the bark of our Cinchona plants originated from the fact that the best Cinchona bark of commerce is invariably overgrown with moss. Hence the supposition that moss preserved the alkaloids from the process of oxidation or deterioration, which they apparently undergo when the bark is long exposed to the full action of light."‡

This is an interesting account of the mental process through which the discovery was originated, and it is to be regretted that in describing it Mr. M'Ivor should have named *moss* instead of *lichen*, the closely-adhering thallus of the various sorts of which does no doubt produce effects similar to those described.§ " Moss " is scarcely ever seen on good barks, except on branches which have trailed along the ground.

Mr. M'Ivor's plan is thus described by himself‖ :—" In removing the strip of bark, two parallel cuts should be made down the stem at the distance apart of the intended width of the strip of bark ; this done, the bark is raised from the sides of the cut and drawn off, beginning from the bottom ; care being taken not to press or injure the sappy matter (*cambium*) left upon the stem of the tree. This *cambium*, or sappy matter, immediately granulates on the removal of the bark, and being covered, forms a new bark, which maintains the circulation undisturbed." Mr. Broughton says in a letter to me (December 27, 1867) :—

Réunion, in Guadaloupe and in Martinique, in Algeria, Rio de Janeiro, St. Helena, the Canaries, and the Azores, at Melbourne in Australia, in the Caucasus,—probably also in other places. Java, British India, and Ceylon, I need not again mention.
 * Taymullay, near Soonda-betta Peak. See Markham's Map of the Neilgherries.
 † See Ill. Nueva Quin. *sub voce Uvitusinga*, p. 3. ‡ Return, etc. (as above), p. 167.
 § And yet lichens *tied upon* the barked trees are injurious, and to be carefully rejected, as generating a fungus which injures the wood of the plants (see the same page). ‖ Return, etc., p. 167.

" If the cambium be not injured, fresh bark seems always rapidly to grow. I have found also the quality improved almost as if by mossing." Let us then in the first place seek to get a clear idea of this cambium, according to the most recent researches into its structure and functions.*

The Cambium.

If we examine the stem of a tree in winter, or during the period of complete rest, we find between the last-formed layer of wood and the bark a layer of cellular tissue. It was formed in the course of the preceding year by the influence of the nourishing sap descending between the bark and the wood. This matter appears at first as if in a liquid state, and constitutes that which is called the cambium, so named first by our countryman Grew, whose quaint, but for the time wonderfully accurate account, I subjoin.† By degrees this cambium becomes organized into a tissue, in which all the phenomena of the growth of the stem in width seem to originate. At the first return of spring the nourishing sap flows abundantly into this generative layer and swells up its component parts. This zone is composed of tolerably regular cellular tissue. Insensibly, by the progress of vegetation, a large number of these cells become longer, their cell-walls thicken, and soon present all the character of fibrous tissue. Coincidently with this transformation, a certain number of cells dispersed in the midst of the others increase in diameter and in length, their walls present transparent punctuation, and they become converted into radiated or punctuated vessels. These vessels and these tubes form bundles separated by a cellular tissue, which keeps its primitive form, and, after some time, all the interior of the generative zone becomes organized into a new woody layer, which adheres to and forms part of the previously-formed wood. At the same time in the portion of the generative layer which is in contact with the bark, a certain number of cells undergo similar transformations, assimilating them to, and preparing them to form a new portion of bark.

The time when the sap thus begins to flow into this generative layer was chosen by M'Ivor as the most favourable for the removal of the bark; it is then easily separated from the wood, and I found the bark thus gathered to be in excellent condition, and rich in alkaloids.‡ This flow of sap takes place at different periods, according to the climate, but there seems to be always a period of rest and of renewed spring of vegetation.

Mode of Renewal of the Bark.

It will thus be seen how important it is to understand thoroughly not only the conditions under which the renewal can be effected, but also the mode in which it takes place. On this point I have not met with any clearer information than is afforded by the celebrated French botanist M. Trécul, in several memoirs presented to the Academy and afterwards published in the ' Annales des Sciences Naturelles.'§

M. Trécul‖ not only furnished new proofs of the co-operation of the wood and the bark in the formation of new annual layers, but also demonstrated—which is very important—that each of these two fundamental parts of the branch, when artificially isolated, may give rise to the production either of wood or of bark.

Messrs. Duhamel, Meyen, and others, had previously asserted that when a portion of the wood of the trunk is laid bare, and that the portion thus decorticated is so ordered as to be preserved from desiccation

---

* Richard, ' Nouveaux Éléments de Botanique,' p. 167.

† " The sap, passing into the cortical body, through this (as through a *Manica Hippocratis*) is still more finely filtered. With which sap the cortical body being dilated as far as its tone, without a solution of continuity, will bear, and the supply of sap still renewed, the purest part, as most apt and ready, recedes with its due tinctures *from the said cortical body to all parts of the lignous*,—both those mixed with the bark and those lying within it. Which lignous body likewise, *superinducing its own proper tinctures into the said sap*, 'tis now to its highest preparation wrought up, and becomes (as they speak of that of an animal) the vegetative *ros* or *cambium*, the noblest part whereof is at last coagulated in and assimilated to the like substance with the same lignous body."—' The Anatomy of Plants, with an Idea of a Philosophical History of Plants,' and several other Lectures, read before the Royal Society, by Nehemiah Grew, M.D., F.R.S., 1682, book i. p. 15.

‡ Report, 353, pp. 181, 182.   § Ann. des Sc. Nat. 1853, t. xix.; ibid. 1854.   ‖ Duchartre, ' Éléments de Botanique,' p. 282.

and from atmospheric influences, there are seen exuding from the surface of the wood, gelatinous protuberances,—*mamelons*, as they were named by Duhamel, or gelatinous drops, as they were called by Meyen.* These productions, after they have become multiplied in number, and extending nearer to each other, at length become hardened and organized as fresh bark. Duhamel looked upon this as an organizable liquid. Meyen noticed that this exudation, from the first moment when it shewed itself at the extremity of the medullary rays, was composed of a very delicate cellular tissue, the cells of which contained a gummy mucilage; but M. Trécul first clearly showed that these new productions are *from the beginning composed of cells*, and that these cells, which have a gelatinous appearance, are produced by those of the generative layer (*couche génératrice*), which remains on the surface after the bark has been removed. It would seem, indeed, that where these have been removed by the abrasion of the whole surface of the wood, renewal of the bark does not take place. It will be seen how strongly these views confirm the practical value of the plan of M'Ivor.†

We have seen that the one special condition of renewal is that the surface of the denuded wood should be constantly kept moist. In the year 1852 M. Trécul submitted to the Academy the trunk of a tree (*Nyssa angulisans*) brought from Louisiana, where it had been protected by the shade of a damp, marshy forest from the direct action of the sun. It had been deprived of its bark for the space of sixteen or seventeen inches all round the stem, and nevertheless not only continued to grow, but bore leaves and fruit. Fresh layers had begun to form, not only in connection with the bark both above and below the decorticated portion, but also on the surface of the wood deprived of its bark. Oblong or hemispherical projections covered with bark of a greyish colour, having as yet no contact with the remaining bark of the tree, grew as represented in the accompanying Plate. Well-executed representations of microscopical sections of these renewed portions are added. *This formation appears to be connected with prolongation of the medullary rays*, and, in addition to a fibro-vascular structure, there are seen, as in the Plate No. 18,‡ *some punctuated and radiated vessels*. The projections themselves partake of the nature of wood rather than bark, in this respect differing from the perfect bark obtained by mossing.

Origin of the Renewed Bark.

As it seems to be demonstrated that the most profitable mode of cultivation will be the renewal of the bark under moss, as described above, it becomes a very important practical question to consider whence the fresh and very rich materials are derived out of which the new bark is elaborated.

In order to arrive at the truth in this matter, it is necessary to pass in review some ascertained facts in reference to the course of those fluids in the plant, by means of which it is nourished and increased. It is through the roots, which are continually extending, and, as it were, going in search of nourishment, that the plant absorbs from the soil a large quantity of water and of common air,—both of which are needful to its existence. It also receives various earthy salts, of which it appears, from the most recent research, to have the power of admitting some and rejecting others.§ As is well expressed by Grew in his 'Anatomy of Plants' (Book i. p. 15), "The contiguous moisture, by the cortical body, being a body laxe and spongy, is easily admitted; yet not all indiscriminately, but that which is more adapted to pass through the surrounding cuticle." The liquid thus absorbed by the roots rises through the fibro-vascular system. It is an essentially watery liquid, and contains only traces of certain principles,—gum,

---

* I have not met with any chemical analysis of this organisable matter, but suspect, from imperfect experiments of my own, that *hydrate of silica* (in some soluble form) plays an important part in it.

† Mr. Broughton writes (March 16, 1868):—"I have long remarked that the bark, when carefully removed without injury to the cambium, quickly renews itself from below, not from the edges. The analysis made of bark so renewed, of six months' growth, has at present corroborated your statement respecting the old practice of the casearilleros." ‡ Sciences Nat. Botanique, 1852.

§ See a very interesting paper, "De la Répartition de la Potasse et de la Soude dans les Végétaux," lu par M. Péligotin, à l'Académie des Sciences, le 4 novembre 1867, 'Annales de Chimie et de Physique.'

D

sugar, albumen, gluten, and other material in solution. But during the progress of vegetation, the proportion of these matters becomes increased, and when the sap has arrived at the extremities of the plant it
contains more organic principles than when collected in the vicinity of the roots. In the trees with soft
wood the ascent of the sap takes place through the whole extent, in others apparently in the sap-wood
only. This, which is generally called the ascending sap, is attracted to the leaves and to all the external
parts of the plant, having in itself, it is said, no power to convey nourishment; but it is submitted in
the leaves, in a very curious and complicated manner, to the action of the atmosphere and of the light,
by means of which most important changes occur: carbonic acid is decomposed and the oxygen driven off;
chlorophyll is elaborated, together with many other less marked products. The sap, which is fraught with
these and now fitted for nutrition, and called the descending or nourishing sap (*sève nourricière*) makes its
way downwards, and is attracted to every part of the plant where its presence is needed, the ordinary
channel for its course being the portion belonging to the outside of the woody structure and internal part
of the bark, in which increase very manifestly takes place at every fresh period of the growth of the plant.
This course of the descending sap may be traced down even to the roots; and, as I have mentioned in
previously published remarks, also laterally by the medullary rays, specially near the base of the stem,
thus furnishing a channel for throwing into the ever-active circulation of the sap some of the substances
which have been elaborated in the bark, and which may be carried by the ascending current to fulfil
important purposes in other regions of the plant.*

If this circulation of the ascending and descending sap be entirely checked, of course the tree perishes;
but there seems to exist considerable adaptability in seeking out fresh channels when the old ones are
partially closed. Thus we familiarly observe old trees, of which the heart-wood has entirely perished,
carrying on a vigorous ascension of the sap through what little may remain adhering to the bark; and, on
the other hand, cases sometimes occur as in the trunk of a celebrated lime-tree at Fontainebleau, (described
in the 'Annales des Sciences' for 1855). This tree was planted in 1780, and in the year 1810 was
deprived of bark round the trunk for a considerable space; and, although this was so far from being
renewed that decay affected the wood to such a depth that the diameter of the tree was at length reduced
by three-quarters, it grew and apparently flourished till the year 1854. In this case the whole circulation
must have been carried on in the centre of the tree, whilst the surface was being destroyed, showing the
power of adaptation to circumstances which exists in the vegetable kingdom. An instance of the same
adaptability, but in an endogenous plant, has just fallen under my notice in an account of the Great
Dragon Tree (*Dracæna Draco*) of Orotava, in Teneriffe, described by Humboldt, which perished in a gale
last autumn. "When I visited it in February," says Signor Fenzi, the writer of the description, "it was
still *in excellent health*,—its immense crown covered with innumerable panicles of scarlet fruits, and the
huge trunk, *although completely decayed in the interior*, sustained vigorously the spreading mass of fleshy
branches and sword-like foliage. Its circumference was about seventy-eight English feet, while the total
height did not exceed seventy-five feet; and it was remarkable that through some crevices in the trunk
a small *Dracæna* was seen growing spontaneously in the decayed substance furnished by the parent-tree."

The sap must in this case have risen for many centuries in the outer portion of the trunk.

Having thus rapidly passed under review some preliminary observations in reference to the circulation
of the sap in plants in general, I now proceed to consider a question which must be looked upon as
practically important in reference to the cultivation of the Quinine-producing plantations in India. I have
found by analysis a steady improvement in the bark renewed over spaces that had been previously
decorticated, having received from Mr. M'Ivor specimens of the first, second, and third time of renewal.
The structure, as exhibited microscopically,† also shows a manifest and gradually perfected building-up of

* Illustr. of Nueva Quin. Micr. Obs. p. 2.
† Mr. Broughton also says (March 16, 1868), "A microscopic examination shows no difference in structure between it and
the mossed bark."

the tissues and component portions of the bark.* This is not more wonderful than many similar facts, both in the animal and vegetable world; but the truly remarkable circumstance is the very large amount of alkaloid found in the bark of the third time of renewal, in a state also easily purified and better fitted for the extraction of Quinine than the bark in its normal condition.

Is this state of things to last and become permanent, so that by continually stripping the trees of portions of their external covering, it should become in the same proportion more rich in the very product that we need? This seems very improbable; and yet it is the conclusion to be arrived at from the above experiments; and even theoretically considered, it may not be so unlikely as at first it appears. If the Quinine, like the chlorophyll, had to be elaborated almost entirely in the leaves, I confess that such a result would seem very unlikely, as it would render a more vigorous condition of the leaves necessary, or else a more abundant production of these respiratory organs of the plant; and it is quite certain that nothing of the sort could happen from the removal of the bark. Moreover, chemical analysis comes in aid of our conjectures, and shows conclusively that the leaves are so far from being a chief seat of the alkaloids that they possess only a trace of these.

Neither can the bark which remains round the decorticated portion be looked upon as the chief source of supply of alkaloids, more particularly since the following experiment of Mr. Broughton seems conclusively to show the contrary, and that, instead of finding an increase in the alkaloids in such a case, the reverse is the fact. In Mr. Broughton's Report for April, 1867, he says:—

"It appeared to me that an examination of the bark that had been renewed by natural processes, without the aid of moss, would possess considerable interest. It was suggested by a statement in Howard's 'Nueva Quinologia of Pavon,' and also given on the authority of Ruiz. I was able to obtain a small quantity of such renewed bark from two *succirubra* trees, which had been injured and partially stripped of their bark by the falling of a log in October, 1864. The renewed bark was thicker than that of the natural bark, measuring 0·19 to 0·22 inch, instead of 0·16, and had replaced itself *mainly from the edges of the wound, not from the surface, as is the case with mossed bark;* but its analysis gave but 5 per cent. of alkaloids, of which about 3·25 appeared to consist of Chinchonidine and Chinchonine."

This experiment seems to me important, as tending to the conclusion that the sap which is conveyed from the adjoining bark does not contain all the materials needful for the abundant production of Quinine and the other alkaloids. Nehemiah Grew was perhaps right in saying "that the concurrence by two specifically distinct fluids is as necessary to nutrition in plants as in animals."† Whence then can the cambium derive these supplies if not from the heart-wood?—a source which, as we have seen by the appearance of the sappy matter at the end of the medullary rays, is already rendered probable.

Mr. Broughton remarks, in a letter dated March 16, 1868, "I have long remarked that the bark, when carefully removed *without injury to the cambium,* quickly renews itself from below, *not from the edge.* The analysis made of bark so renewed, of six months' growth, has at present corroborated your statement respecting the old practice of the cascarilleros, as being richer in alkaloid than the original."

Mr. M'Ivor writes,‡ "the new bark rises direct from the sap-wood if the old bark is carefully removed; *in three days the new bark is formed entirely over the whole surface, i. e.* rising directly from the sap [wood], and not formed by a current of cambium from under the remaining bark; as, in the general opinion, is the manner in which all wounds are repaired."

The Heart-wood.

The heart-wood comes next in review as a possible source of alkaloid. My attention was directed to the examination of it for Quinine by a letter from Mr. Broughton, in which he mentions, in the following

* "Les jeunes tissus végétaux, ceux de la couche génératrice en particulier, ont la propriété de se modifier, de se métamorphoser pour produire tel ou tel organe dans telle ou telle situation, suivant les besoins de la plante."—*Trécul, Ann. des Sciences Naturelles,* tome xvii. 1852, p. 276.　　† 'The Anatomy of Plants,' book iii. p. 131.　　‡ In Letter, 3rd June, 1868.

terms, his discovery of Quinine in the wood of *C. succirubra:*—"The most interesting point I have ascertained lately is the presence of alkaloid in the older heart-wood of the Red-bark tree. This amounts to 0·10 per cent of the weight of the wood. I have obtained it as a crystalline sulphate. The most remarkable instance is that of a tree which, though rich in alkaloids, contained no Quinine, but Quinidine. To my great surprise, *the whole of the wood-alkaloid was Quinine.*"

Now, since the weight of wood is to that of the bark as (perhaps on the average) 10 to 1, we should, in such case, be at once furnished with a kind of inexhaustible storehouse of alkaloids for the renewed bark, and should have discovered the very thing of which we were in search.

In order to obtain further information on this point, and to trace the results of the flow of sap as above described, I took some portions remaining of a Red-bark tree, part of which was sent me in the year 1860 from the Mountain Chahuarpata, in the Province of Alausi (South America), and which I have elsewhere described,* subjecting them to examination as below.

Root of Red-bark tree, 10 inches in diameter, solid, heavy, almost like box-wood:—

1.—1750 grains, acted upon by distilled water and a warm temperature for several days. The loss of weight, 25 per cent., consisting of water, gum, some impure Kinova-bitter, with oxidized colouring-matter, and combined with a trace of alkaloid.

I use the term Kinova-bitter as a name for this glycoside, which is not pure kinovic acid. (See my Illustr. Nuov. Quin. *sub voce C. magnifolia.*)

2.—The remainder, fully dried, was submitted to the action of ether, which formed a light yellow solution, which, evaporated, left 0·10 per cent. of the substance previously described as "Cinchotannic acid" or "mother-substance" (described further on).

3.—The residuary portion was acted on by spirit of wine, which dissolved out an additional 0·17 per cent. of the above substance (making, with that before mentioned, 0·270 per cent. of the wood examined), together with 0·330 of oxidizable resin, some part of which (when the above substance had been separated by ether) would not again dissolve in spirit, appearing to have been changed into humus. A similar change took place on the addition of solution of permanganate of potash to the mother-substance.

4.—Another portion, 3500 grains, was subjected to the action of lime-water, the filtered solution precipitated by hydrochloric acid, the Kinova-bitter dissolved in spirit of wine (and thus separated from about 1 per cent. of oxidized colouring-matter), and then evaporated, gave 1·60 per cent.

5.—A portion of the woody fibre was calcined and examined by my son, W. D. Howard, with the following result. The proportion of ash to weight of wood was 0·55 per cent., consisting of—

Carbonate of lime	0·121
Carbonate of potash	0·159
Carbonate of manganese	0·031
Silica	0·097
Phosphates of iron and alumina, and peroxide of iron	0·062
Loss and undetermined, which includes some carbonate of soda	0·080
	0·550

6.—3500 grains, as above, were treated for the extraction of the alkaloids, and yielded 1·00 per cent. of rough and impure precipitated alkaloid, which partially dissolved in ether; the addition of oxalic acid to this solution did not cause a crystallization, and the Quinine present appeared to be in a peculiar state. I did not succeed in this experiment in getting a quantitative result; the next was more successful.

7.—Another portion, of 3500 grains, gave, of alkaloids soluble in ether, per cent.

Quinine and Cinchonidine	0·41
Cinchonicine	0·05
	0·46

In both these experiments the presence of the peculiar resin, elsewhere described, to the extent of at least 1 per cent. of the wood, rendered crystallization of the sulphates difficult.

In order to follow the course of the ascending sap, I took a portion of the stem-wood of the same tree, measuring about 23 inches in circumference, and having split off the outside till the circumference

---

* See Illustr. Nuov. Quin. *sub voce C. succirubra,* p. 4.

was reduced to 18 inches, I examined the two portions separately, first the heart-wood, and then the more external ligneous portion, as under:—

1.—Heart-wood, 3500 grains in powder acted on by lime-water, and, as above (No. 4), gave of Kinova-bitter 1·13. This was not implicated with so much colouring-matter as in the root-wood.

2.—3500 grains, examined for alkaloids, gave—

Soluble in ether—Quinine, etc.	0·10
Soluble in spirits of wine—Cinchonine	0·03
„ „ „ Do., with resinous or colouring-matter*	...?
	0·13

3.—Outside wood of stem. 3500 grains, treated as above for Kinova-bitter, gave (after separation by spirits of wine of a trace of colouring-matter), Kinova-bitter, 1·20 per cent.

4.—Examined for alkaloids, gave—

Soluble in ether—Quinine, etc.	0·09
Soluble in spirits of wine—Cinchonine	0·03
„ „ „ Do. with resinous matter*	...?
	0·12

Showing apparently a trifling increase in the kinova-bitter, and *possibly* a corresponding slight diminution in the proportion of alkaloid towards the outside of the wood.

In order further to examine the stem-wood, I took another portion (of 7000 grains), without separating the outer and inner bark. This enabled me to check the results previously obtained, and also, as being a larger quantity examined, to carry out more fully the purification and separation of the alkaloids, which, in such small quantities, is proportionally difficult.

1.—7000 grains were treated with ether for extraction of the mother-substance, of which nearly 2 per cent. of the weight of the wood was obtained.

2.—The remaining woody fibre, digested with water, gave, of gum, kinate of lime, and some colouring-matter, not quite 2 per cent. of the weight of the wood.

3.—The remainder, digested with lime-water (and as above), gave, of Kinova bitter, implicated with 0·05 colouring-matter, 1·138.

4.—The remainder examined for alkaloids gave, as a rough precipitate, 0·37 per cent., or, as refined, 0·171, after separation of some adherent resin (chiefly) and wax, but also loss of alkaloid, as it had been very carefully purified; and, on solution in ether and addition of oxalic acid, gave a good crystallization of oxalate of Quinine.

Quinine	0·043
Cinchonidine†	0·030
Quinidine,‡ and soluble Cinchonine§	0·041
Cinchonine‖	0·033
Cinchonicine	0·024
Total	0·171

---

* Very impure. † Separated as hydriodate.

‡ Crystallizes as hydriodate; gives fine characteristic crystals from ether, and a green colour with chlorine and ammonia.

§ Under the head "Soluble Cinchonine" I include provisionally an alkaloid near to Cinchonine, but quite soluble in ether at 0·730, at ordinary temperatures. As I was desirous of having the opinion of Dr. Hernpath, especially about its iodo-sulphate, I forwarded this gentleman a small quantity, from which he obtained the following results, in accordance with mine (as far as these latter went):—

1st. It crystallizes in long, rectangular prisms, having bihedral summits.

2nd. It furnishes a highly fluorescent sulphate in solution, having the same optical effects as Quinine and Quinidine, as far as the epipolic dispersion is concerned.

3rd. It gives, with chlorine and ammonia, a white precipitate, without any trace of the green of Quinine and Quinidine.

4th. It does not form an iodo-sulphate on a plate of glass, Quinine does (even if first made into a sulphate), but amorphous resin only.

5th. By spontaneous evaporation of a solution in a tube it furnishes black *aciculæ*, having a purplish reflection, almost all opaque, but when thin enough to transmit colour, intensely blood-red; but very thin plates transmitted a deep brown-yellow.

6th. It is probably a new modification of Cinchonine, differing by a molecule of water from (*Huanokis?*) Compare the *two Cinchonidins.* (Ann. d. Ph. und der Ch. 1863, p. 325.)

‖ Separated from the residuary liquor, insoluble in ether; soluble in and crystallizes from spirits of wine.

E

It follows, from these experiments,[*] that the Mother-substance can be separated without any interference with or diminution of the weight of the kinova-bitter.

Also, that the alkaloids must be in a state of combination rendering them insoluble in water, as there was no evidence of their presence in any quantity in the gummy solution, which gave a brown, oily sublimate by Grähe's test. This agrees with the probability of their existing as combined with kinovic acid, and not with kinic acid, of which last the traces were very faint. Ammonia, in some combination, was very manifestly present.

I was surprised to find Quinidine well ascertained in the stem-wood, but, on referring to what I before published,[†] I see that I obtained Quinidine crystallizing as hydriodate from the inner and not from the outer bark, which shows a coincidence that can scarcely be accidental. In my present examination of the bark of *C. Almaguerensis* (which resembles red bark) I notice a similar result.

The heart-wood of young plants of *C. succirubra*, sent me by Mr. M'Ivor, in 1863, gave me an opportunity of examining the results of eighteen months' growth. Here there was not yet the true compact ligneous structure; and, on examination, I was unable to detect any of the mother-substance above mentioned, but kinova-bitter, gum, and some chlorophyll were present. The presence of the latter shows the immature condition of the wood in these specimens, which were gathered during a season of much rain, and in the full flow of the sap. I did not recognize in them any alkaloid.

The Leaves.

The leaves come next in the course of the ascending sap, and it is in these that we may expect to find its constituent principles more concentrated. We have to consider, in connection with these, the results of their exposure to the atmospheric influence, the fixation of carbon, the throwing off of oxygen under the influence of the light of the sun,—in a word, the well-known processes of vegetable assimilation and growth. I find in the leaves—ammonia, in some combination, abundant; chlorophyll in the second modification described by Berzelius, which, in combination with hydrochloric acid, gives a most lovely emerald colour,—a valuable dye, if it could be fixed in that state. It is indeed, as remarked by Berzelius, to be ranked amongst dyeing substances, though not amongst those giving fast colours. I also find the xanthophyll of Berzelius, and perhaps another modification of chlorophyll, which, under the influence of chlorine, gives rise to red and pink colours, such as are visible in the fading leaf.

I first showed the presence of alkaloids in the leaf in the following Report, given in June, 1863 :—

"The absence of any carmine sublimate by heat[‡] led me at first to an unfavourable conclusion. The decoctions and infusions made by M'Ivor, though in perfectly good condition, showed that the contents changed most rapidly under the influence of the oxygen of the atmosphere, as soon as ammonia was added to the, at first, decidedly acid liquor. Fortunately, a good supply of several ounces of dried leaves had been sent over, and from these I succeeded in obtaining Quinine, though in very small quantity, but presenting its usual characteristics . . . but nevertheless showing a characteristic implication with resinous or extractive matter, such as is usually met with in the very smallest quills or canutillos of South American bark, in analysing which it is frequently difficult to purify the Quinine from this adhesion. I obtained first from these leaves to the extent of 0·11 of alkaloid, of which part was soluble in ether, the remainder in spirits of wine, and afterwards, 0·19 of precipitate, still more combined with

* Another examination of stem-wood gave, by different process,—

(Quinine?) alkaloid soluble in ether, sp. gr. 0·714	.	0·129
Cinchonidine (soluble in ether, sp. gr. 0·730)	. .	0·029
Cinchonine (and Quinidine?) . . .	.	0·070
Cinchonicine	.	0·029
		0·257

The total amount is here more correct than in No. 4, as there was less loss of alkaloid soluble in ether. The qualitative estimate better in the above.

† 'Microscopical Observations,' p. 6.   ‡ Grähe's test (Chemisches Centralblatt), March, 1860.

astringent matter. From these data, it seems to follow that the leaves will not supply a material for the extraction of Quinine, but that they will nevertheless be very useful when used fresh or in recently prepared decoction or infusion for the cure of the fevers of the country."

Towards the end of June, 1863, Dr. Anderson, of the Botanic Gardens, Calcutta, began, with Dr. Simpson, to examine chemically the nature of the leaves of *C. succirubra*, and reports, on the 25th July, having obtained "little needle-shaped crystals in a fluid obtained from the leaves of the Cinchona." In a subsequent letter, dated the 7th August of the same year, Dr. Anderson says, "I have the honour to inform you that I have to-day received intelligence from England of the discovery of Quinine in small quantities in the leaves of Cinchona sent from this country. Quinine obtained from the leaves was exhibited by Mr. Howard, at the meeting of the Linnean Society, London, on the 18th June, 1863."

In December of the same year, I gave a further report on the leaves, which I subjoin :—

"Several pounds' weight of leaves (well dried, and with a marked tea-like fragrance) have allowed me the opportunity of following various lines of experiment in order to ascertain their probable commercial value. I regret to be obliged to confirm the opinion I expressed in my last, that the leaves will not supply material for the extraction of Quinine, although the quantity of the first rough precipitate from an acid solution—having the appearance of a hydrated alkaloid—is considerably more than I succeeded in obtaining before, being equal to 1·31 per cent. of the weight of the leaves. Of this, a small portion was soluble in ether to the extent of 0·17 per cent.,* forming a clear yellow solution, which precipitates on the addition of a solution of oxalic acid in spirit of wine. Nevertheless, the further prosecution of the inquiry, and the attempt to purify the alkaloid, showed me clearly that I had to do with a state of things *very different from that which existed in the bark*, and that I should not succeed in obtaining an available salt of Quinine."

I remark further that "the alkaloid exists in the leaves in very intimate relationship with the green colouring-matter" (chlorophyll), and this is important in reference to the present investigation, for if the leaves were called upon for a fresh flow of sap, descending at once to where the denuded portion of the wood called for fresh clothing, it is but reasonable to suppose we should find something of the same very marked peculiarity,—as is, indeed, always characteristic of the bark of the young twigs, which stand next to the leaves in the nature of their product, as they do also in course of the sap circulation. So far from anything like this being the case, we have markedly the reverse characters; indeed, the presence of chlorophyll (though so important an element in the vigour of the plant) seems not correlative with that of the alkaloids, and it is entirely absent in the rich renewed bark of the *C. succirubra* as received from the East Indies.

Dr. Herapath has found optical results of very considerable interest arise from examination of the above constituents of the leaves; especially an alcoholic solution of the chlorophyll which I sent him gave in the spectroscope extraordinary results, agreeing with the properties of chlorophyll from the leaves of hyoscyamus, digitalis, tea, senna, and some other plants. Dr. Herapath remarks truly, "There must be some cause why solutions which have such equally green tints to the eye should present such different optical effects, and the most probable is the existence of different substances in these leaves."

Course of the Ascending Sap.

Next to the leaves come the very small twigs, which seem to partake more of the character impressed by the ascending than that of the descending sap. I quote as an illustration from my report (June, 1864) on "Bark from the spray or small portions of the same branches as No. 1:"—"From this I did not succeed in obtaining more than 0·90 per cent. of impure alkaloid, which lost one-half in the attempt to purify, since the alkaloids are much implicated with tannin (apparently) and not capable of easy crystallization."

---

* In April, 1867, Mr. Broughton reports that from four pounds of the leaves of *C. succirubra* he "succeeded in obtaining 3·10 grains of alkaloid, of which about one grain was soluble in ether, and gave a faint indication of Quinine when tested with chlorine-water and ammonia."

It will be seen that this amount (= 0·45) coincides almost exactly with the product obtained from the wood of the roots, which I have given above as Quinine and Cinchonidine, 0·41; and Cinchonicine, 0·05; together, 0·46.

The increase in alkaloid in the bark of the larger branches *of the same tree* (sent as No. 1) was remarkable. These gave, of *purified alkaloids*, per cent.—

Quinine . . .		3·14
Cinchonidine .		2·06
Cinchonine .	.	0·80
		6·00

I think I may fairly consider that in this latter case of the larger branches the descending sap must have come into play, together with the cell-formation of the cambium, as elsewhere described.

The Alkaloids formed in the Bark.

We have thus far traced the deposits of the ascending sap in its course from the roots, through the wood, to the leaves; and we do not find any reason to look upon either the wood of the roots, or of the stem, or of the more succulent and recently-formed portions of the ligneous structure as the seat of the formation of the alkaloids. In all these parts the proportion of alkaloid is insignificant when compared with that of the bark. In the root-wood, moreover, it is found in such a state as would naturally follow from its being deposited there (as combined with resin, which is a secondary and not a primary product of vegetation) after its downward course, such as I have described,[*] is completed, and then carried laterally from the root-bark by the medullary rays into the root-wood. In the outside portion of the stem-wood we find rather less alkaloid and rather more kinovic acid than in the centre-wood, and there is a smaller amount of resin, but a perhaps larger proportion of wax[†] associated with the alkaloids: they exist, in both, in a somewhat greater degree of purity than in the root.

When we come to the leaves, we find almost the same proportion of alkaloid as in the wood, but this amount not increased, as would surely be the case if the leaves were the seat of its formation. Nothing seems changed, except that here we find (as also in the very young wood) the presence of chlorophyll, which in the descent of the sap, appears gradually to degenerate in the bark of the small twigs into, or else to become mixed with, a tannin substance, and this again into resin. In tracing the course of the nourishing or descending sap, we find the alkaloids increasing *greatly*—not less than ten- or twentyfold, often much more—in their relative amount in the liber, as compared with the parts we have passed under review; and what is also very important, they are in a state of much greater purity, as if freshly formed. In the cellular envelope there is again a considerable increase, to the extent of 100 or 150 per cent. on the contents of the liber, and the alkaloids, or at least Quinine and Cinchonidine appear to be especially stored up in this cellular envelope, but this in connection ordinarily with various substances difficult to separate from them. In the mossed barks, and also, according to Dr. De Vrij, in the root-bark of the young plants of *C. Pahudiana*, from some cause—possibly from the absence of sunlight—the alkaloids seem to exist in the cellular envelope in a state of greater purity.

The review of the whole seems to point to the *bark* as the seat of the formation of the alkaloid.

In my 'Illustrations of the Nueva Quinologia'[‡] I gave it as my opinion that the alkaloids were gradually formed, chiefly in the bark itself, and to this view (founded on practical observation of the increase of the proportion of alkaloid in the increasingly developed bark) I now return as the result of the more extended researches in the present volume.

---

* Illustr. Nuev. Quin. Microscop. Obs. p. 2.   † Cerotic acid (saponifying with alkalies).
‡ 'Microscopical Observations,' p. 2.

Ascending and Descending Sap.

The following Table presents in a concise form the result of the flow of the ascending and of the descending sap on the production of alkaloids:—

	Quinine.	Cinchoni-dine.	Quinidine.	Cinchonine.	Cincho-nicine and Sol. Cinc.	Total per cent.
	Ascending Sap.					
Root-wood (Chahuarpata-tree) . .	0·410		. .	0·050	. .	0·460
Stem-wood (do.)	0·043	0·030	0·041	0·033	0·024	0·171
Leaves	*	*	*	. .	*	0·170
Twigs	*	*	*	. .	*	0·450
	Descending Sap.					
"Canuto" of large branches . . .	3·140	2·060	.	0·800	.	6·000
Bark of (4-inch diam.) branch of Chahuar-pata-tree	2·940	1·350	. .	0·860	0·0250	5·175
Trunk (bark):—(a) liber or inner bark* .	2·380	1·200	. .	0·560	0·130	4·270
(b) cellular envelope	6·400	1·900	. .	0·760	0·200	9·260
(c) first harvest of renewed bark .	{3·750 / 0·900?}	*	.	*	1·80	6·450
(d) second harvest of renewed bark .	6·340	1·140	. .	*	0·20	10·60?
(e) third harvest of renewed bark .	{4·610 / 2·000?}	1·140	. .	. .	0·053	11·20?
Root-bark, from Mr. Broughton's Report .	2·150		3·850		. .	6·000
Root-bark, Author's analysis . . .	{1·031 / 4·050?}	trace	trace	3·000	3·940?	12·750?
Do. De Vrij's analysis . .	4·031?	trace	. .	7·440?		11·750

It will be seen that the twigs and the root-wood agree in their alkaloidal contents, and also the stem-wood and the leaves. The Quinine has diminished, and the Cinchonine increased as the sap draws towards the root. The Chahuarpata Red-bark-tree is the one previously described from Alausi.

Influence of Respiration.

The *respiration* of plants did not escape the acute observation and profound research of Nehemiah Grew, who says, in his epistle dedicatory to Charles II., that "even a plant lives partly upon aer, for the reception whereof it hath those parts which are answerable to lungs." The idea thus felicitously conceived has since been brought, by the researches of many observers, within the domain of actual science. In fact, the access of air to the internal portions of the plant, or in other words, its respiration, is so important to its welfare that it is found to be provided for in three distinct methods :—First, by the roots absorbing air, together with water, from the soil.† This has been compared by Bouchardat‡ to the functions of the *branchiæ* or gills in fishes, and is so needful that plants often perish from this supply being interfered with, as when, for example, a depth of earth is heaped over the roots of a tree. Secondly, by the curiously contrived *stomata* which constitute true respiratory organs of the leaves, analogous to the lungs in plants. Thirdly, by the vessels, reticulated or otherwise, which, having served the purpose of the conveyance of sap in the first spring of circulation, become gradually filled with air, and form channels of respiration, subjecting the fluids

---

* See p. 23, and also the Appendix.   The (?) indicates a deduction of uncertain amount to be made for water, etc.   The weight of acid, etc., is elsewhere in this table deducted.

† The experiments of Th. de Saussure prove that plants perish in a few days, if their roots are surrounded with hydrogen, with azote, or especially with carbonic acid, whilst they continue to live a long time if surrounded by common air.   This botanist has also shown that oxygen, absorbed by the roots, forms carbonic acid in the interior of the vegetable, and at the expense of the latter ; also, that if a root isolated from the stem is placed under experiment, the quantity of oxygen absorbed by it from the air does not exceed the volume of this organ ; whilst, if a root attached to the plant is under examination, the absorption of gas becomes *much more considerable.*"—*Duchartre,* 'Éléments de Botanique,' p. 234.

‡ 'Recherches sur la Végétation,' Paris, 1846, p. 153.

F

of all parts in which they are found to the vivifying action of the air they convey.* This is compared to the manner in which insects are supplied with air through the *tracheæ* which pervade their bodies. It has hence been called the *trachean respiration.*†

The general result is that the sap experiences modifications which change its nature. By *transpiration* it loses a portion of the water of which it was composed; by varied *secretions* it throws off certain products useless or foreign to its nutrition; and by its contact with atmospheric air—that is, its respiration—it acquires new properties, being converted into a fluid which descends from the leaves towards the roots, constituting what has been called the *descending* or, more properly still, the *nourishing sap,*‡ which seems to be attracted towards any part of the plant where special need exists for its services, as in the case we are here considering of the renewal of the bark after decortication.

As I have chiefly to treat of this kind of respiration which appears to be constantly going forward, though it has sometimes been named *nocturnal respiration,* and which supplies oxygen to the plant, I shall adopt for it the more correct term of *general respiration* ;§ in opposition to that peculiar respiration of the leaves and other green portions of the plant, by virtue of which, under the influence of sunlight, the carbonic acid of the air is decomposed, carbon is fixed, oxygen is disengaged, and the growth of the plant ensured. This latter has been named the *chlorophyllian respiration,* and on it all vegetable organization seems *primarily* to depend. Leaves, when once thoroughly exsiccated, lose the power of decomposing carbonic acid, and no restoration of water will renew this action.‖ The leaf, thus dried, dies, *because it ceases to breathe ;* it is possible to kill it by suspending its respiration (by means of an artificial atmosphere of azote or some other gases) for a sufficient time, and that without the cells being injured, without elimination of the water essential to its organization, without any perceptible modification of the green colouring-matter. This is the *asphyxia* of leaves.¶

Researches of M. Decaisne.

In connection with these researches I heard of a work of M. J. Decaisne** on Madder which at once engaged my attention, as having myself studied the red colouring-matter of this plant, whilst occupied more particularly with that of the *C. succirubra.* I found, as I expected, considerable analogy, though not identity, between the two, as was to be looked for in plants so nearly allied botanically. I did not then pursue the subject : but when I read M. Decaisne's elaborate and very complete treatise, I was charmed not only with the clear and lucid style which, in common with his compatriots, he knows how to apply to scientific subjects, but also with the details of the investigation ; throwing, as it seems to me, much light on the question, and, though published many years ago, not equalled, to my knowledge, by anything that has since been given to the public. He says, in the commencement of his preface, that he considered many of the principal facts and phenomena which he had to study might be explained by the knowledge acquired respecting the respiration of vegetables, and consequently the facts thus established became the point of departure of his experiments. The theory of the coloration of plants is dependent on the knowledge of the functions of the leaves, which are themselves pretty generally the seat of this coloration ; and as the action of light exercises great influence on the respiration, which again is ultimately connected with the phenomena of the immediate principles of vegetables, he thought it was needful to study the action on the

---

* A. Richard, 'Nouveaux Éléments de Botanique,' Paris, 1864, p. 152.

† M. Dutrochet ascertained by experiment that the air contained in the different parts of the plant underwent a change in proportion to its distance from the orifices in the leaves, through which it must enter ; as it circulates in the pneumatic vessels it loses a portion of its oxygen, which is absorbed by the sap in proportion as it traverses the vegetable tissue. (A. Richard, *ut supra*, p. 157.) Thus the air contained in the stem of the water-lily showed only sixteen parts of oxygen in a hundred, and that in the roots, only eight in a hundred.

‡ Duchartre, 'Éléments,' p. 716.   § Duchartre, *ut supra*, p. 751.

‖ Boussingault, " Étude sur les fonctions des feuilles " (Ann. de Chimie et de Physique, mars 1868, p. 333).

¶ Id. p. 359.   ** 'Recherches anatomiques et physiologiques sur la Garance.'

colouring-matter of the most powerful and universally extended principles, viz. light, air, and water, when applied to the plant in different degrees of intensity. M. Decaisne thought that he ought not to limit this examination to the root of the madder, although it is this specially which is the depository of the colouring-matter so important in the arts. "All the parts of the same vegetable," he rightly says, "are tributary '*solidaires*') the one to the other in their action, whether growing in the air or in the earth; and we only completely know the action of the one when the others have been carefully studied in their various aspects."*

The Plant an Organized Whole.

This is the conclusion to which I have also been brought—indeed, I might almost say—compelled to come; so that I place no faith in any of the theories of vegetation which isolate the different parts of the plant; but I agree with Kant, in what seems to me a clear definition, that "the cause of the particular mode of existence of a living body resides *in the whole*," and with Müller, from whose Physiology† I quote, that "there is in living or organic matter a principle constantly in action the operations of which are in accordance with a rational plan, so that the individual parts which it creates in the body are adapted to the design of the whole, and this it is which distinguishes organism."

I do not hold myself called upon to attempt to define the entity of that living principle or typical idea in the plant, of which nevertheless it seems to me to be needful to assume the existence, in order to understand the complete contrast which prevails between the totality of the phenomena of organization and those of crystallization.

There are in nature mysteries beyond the domain of science. Investigation fails, and all our study ends in this, that the invisible things of the great Artificer, even his eternal power and Godhead, are clearly seen by the things that are made. Therefore I consider with an author previously quoted‡, that "Nature and the causes and reasons of things, duly contemplated, naturally lead us unto God, and is one way of securing our veneration of Him." I also judge that "We may as well deny what God hath made *to be*, as what he hath spoken *to be true*, because we understand not *how*." I have no knowledge, for instance, how the *causa causans* gives rise to the *causa causata*, but I am assured that the acknowledgment of the great First Cause is essential to our forming any correct notion of secondary causes, or of the "laws of nature," as we *figuratively* speak.

It is, then, to the operation of this principle, which I may call the life of the plant, that I am obliged to trace the perfect re-establishment of the bark, with all its complicated parts and functions, over the places from which it has been removed by Mr. M'Ivor's process. I compared this at first—as, indeed, the first specimens sent seemed to justify—to the granulation of flesh over the surface of a wound, but the accompanying drawings under the microscope show the bark in the third time of renewal to be *perfectly* renewed, as is the case in the parts replaced by animals of low organization, as the claw, for instance, is formed again after being lost by the lobster.

The distinguished botanist M. Trécul remarks, "Not only do the elements of tissues thus denuded give rise by successive divisions to new formations, but they also undergo the most remarkable transformations to the same end; so that the woody fibre, the parenchyma of the medullary rays, and even vessels of small diameter, become metamorphosed into cellular tissue, the cells of which then become multiplied in their turn, and not only so, but this ordinary cellular tissue reproduces in its turn *new medullary rays, new*

---

* The vitality or growing power of plants seems to be pretty equally distributed throughout their entire structure. If destitute of any great visible centre of life, almost every portion of them, from the largest stem to the smallest bud, seems endowed with the power of establishing independent centres for itself. This potency and general diffusion of life-power enable each part of a plant to assist, and to act and react upon every other portion; hence, if the top suffers loss, the roots make haste to make it good. In a similar way, if the roots are injured or removed, the top at once ministers to their healing and renewed production.—*The Gardeners' Chronicle, July 4th, 1868.*

† Vol. i. p. 19.   ‡ See Grew's 'Anatomy of Plants,' ii. 70.

ligneous fibre, new punctuated vessels (reticulated or spheroidal), new laticiferous ducts." I have noticed in my Microseopical Observations on the Barks of the Cinchonæ that a similar metamorphosis takes place of all the constituents of the bark into cork as the vessels become pressed towards the surface.

I have now to refer to the accompanying drawings by Tuffen West, F.L.S., of sections of Bark from the East Indies, to show the complete reproduction of the substance of the bark, with all its parts in normal order and relationship to each other, and that nothing is wanting, only that the liber fibres are less numerous as being less necessary to strengthen the bark (thus shielded by the moss) against external influences, and consequently " the renewed bark is not so heavy as original bark," as I am informed by M'Ivor.

Looking upon the plant as an organized whole, it is not surprising that from its earliest development it should manifest some of its peculiar characteristics. This M. Decaisne found was the case with the madder, for in the first days of germination, and when the plant was not provided with any other leaves than its two cotyledons, it already contained the same sap, capable of acquiring a reddish tint from the air, which distinguishes the plant, and it followed, as the result of the experiments of this botanist, " that all the immediate principles obtained from the roots of the madder are but the chemical combinations of *one only product*, spread unequally through the whole vegetable."

This statement may possibly require some modification, but on the whole it contains the germ of much truth. I have in a previous work expressed a similar opinion as regards the most characteristic products of the Red-bark-tree in the early stages of growth. I cannot distinguish any remarkable peculiarity in the sap of the plant. It soon oxidizes and turns brown, it is true, but the full development of its peculiarities is reserved for a later stage of growth.[*] Nevertheless, I believe that the characteristic features of the plant are owing fundamentally to *one* substance. Indeed, when we consider the evident fact that all the complex products of the vegetable world (to say nothing of the animal, although so dependent on the vegetable) are built up out of a few simple substances, it must necessarily appear probable that the complexity is in a certain sense more apparent than real, as depending more upon the different arrangement than the actual diversity of the elementary materials. The aliments of plants must always be either liquid or soluble or gaseous ; such only are capable of being taken up by the plant, either by its spongioles or through the stomata. All the solid parts, including even the wonder-working cell-structure, must then have originated in fluid,—*water* being both the means of conveyance of nutriment, and itself forming by far the larger proportion of most plants. Out of six simple non-metallic bodies—oxygen, carbon, hydrogen, nitrogen, sulphur, and phosphorus,—with the addition of the metallic—potassium, calcium, magnesium, and iron,—the whole *Cosmos* of vegetable growth around us takes its rise. It is doubtful whether any other elements[†] are absolutely indispensable to vegetation. To follow out, therefore, M. Decaisne's idea that the peculiar principle of the madder is *one*, we must reflect that the red colour which is so useful in the arts[‡] is a chemical phenomenon totally independent of life. On the contrary, the yellow colour appears to be the result of a vital action which hinders the other, and "*depends on the membranes of the cells.*" To distinguish, then, between the yellow and the red products, is simply to follow the changes of *one substance* from its original formation through its different degrees of oxidation, or, in other words, of its degeneracy.

I have shown that the case is quite similar in reference to the Red-bark, that no red colour exists, in fact, in the living tree, except as it is modified in the flowers, and in the fading leaves or bracts, or in

---

* Pavon says respecting these, " In arborum corticumque amputatione, succum lacteum primum profluit : postea in colorem intense rubicundum transmutatur."

Spruce says, in a paper read before the Linnean Society, December 14, 1859, that his first care was to verify a report that had been made to him by the collectors, to the effect that the tree (*C. succirubra*) had milky juice. This appeared strange and incredible in the Natural Order Rubiaceæ. When a slit was made in the bark by a cutlass, it soon appeared that the sap is actually colourless, but the instant it is exposed to the air it turns white, and in a few minutes afterwards red. The more rapidly this change is effected, and the deeper the ultimate tinge assumed, the more precious is the bark presumed to be.

† My belief is that molecules of *water* enter *as such* into composition of organic structure, as well as oxygen and hydrogen, in atomic combination. I hesitate, therefore, whether I should not add this to the elements.   ‡ 'Recherches,' p. 19.

the bark, especially when old and weathered; that it is the original yellowish mother-substance found in the heart-wood which turns pink or brick-red in the bark, under the influence of the oxygen of the air, especially when assisted by the presence of earth and alkalies, and that the various products, including perhaps the alkaloid, are derived or rather built up from this under the influence of the respiration of the plant. By the respiration of the plant, in this instance, I mean specially the *general* respiration, in opposition to the *chlorophyllian* respiration. The object of this latter is to fix carbon for the development of the plant, and is, of course, quite essential to its vigour and even to its existence; but I have long suspected that the development of the alkaloids and of Quinine, more particularly, did not stand in any special relation to the vigour of the plant; that in fact, where this was impeded, as in very great elevations, where more especially the plant had to clothe itself with much cellular tissue, there was Quinine the most abundant; the explanation being that the cellular tissue is the place of deposit for the peculiar products of the plant, as I have shown in my examination of the internal and external bark. I now proceed to notice one more fact connected with M. Decaisne's researches on madder, which seems to have analogy with the point I am considering. It appears that the cultivators of madder were in the habit of covering up with earth those portions of the stalk of the plant in which they wished to develope the peculiar colouring-matter in place of the chlorophyll, in order to add these etiolated stalks to the roots, in which alone the colouring-matter is found to perfection. M. Decaisne observed,[*] in examining microscopically the cellular tissue, that the cells of the root secrete a yellow liquid, whilst those of the stalk, which are to all appearance identical, become filled with green colouring-matter; and he proposed to himself this question, "Is this so great difference in the secretions, the invariable result of the tissue of the roots, as is the case in certain plants, or does the influence of external agents contribute to reproduce this phenomenon on other parts of the vegetable?" Well-devised experiments showed that it is possible to change at discretion the production of chlorophyll into the elaboration of colouring-matter similar to that of the roots. It happens in this case that the green portions which, when exposed to light, absorb the carbonic acid of the air whilst disengaging oxygen, thus augmenting the quantity of carbon which the plant contains, absorb, on the contrary, in darkness, a part of the oxygen of the atmosphere which surrounds them and replace it with carbonic acid.

This singularly interesting investigation may perhaps throw some light on the manner in which Mr. M'Ivor is able—apparently by causing the *general* to take the place of the *chlorophyllian* respiration—to cause the plants to produce alkaloids of a better quality, and more easily purified from green and other colouring-matters. It suggests the question, Whether the plant may not really produce alkaloid instead of chlorophyll? It is by shrouding the bark of the plant in darkness and moisture that the madder is compelled to produce red colouring-matter instead of chlorophyll. It is by a like process that the Red-bark-tree is made to produce a richer and better bark in the process of M'Ivor.

These facts suggest the idea that in connection with the above change in the respiration, under the influence of the presence or the withdrawal of light, there may be a change in the electrical state, and hence in the chemical activities of the cells themselves, so that the same cells, which under one set of conditions produce one result, under the stimulus of the ray of light, may produce other combinations.

M. Cailletet remarks in a recent paper[†] that, " the calorific rays, as well as the chemical rays, are without action on the strange decomposition of carbonic acid by vegetables, which takes place under conditions altogether different from those which we know how to produce in our laboratories; but the forces which determine this decomposition act upon the elements of this compound body dissolved in the liquids of the leaf, and *we must confess our entire ignorance of the state these elements are in when in*

---

[*] 'Recherches,' p. 22.

[†] " De l'influence des divers rayons colorés sur la décomposition de l'acide carbonique par les plantes," par M. L. Cailletet (' Journal de Pharmacie et de Chimie,' Oct. 1867).

G

solution. It seems . . . that the coloured rays of light which are the most active, in a chemical point of view, are those which least favour the decomposition of carbonic acid."

Since writing the above, I have met with a paper by M. Boussingault* which seems strongly to confirm the views I have expressed. He shows that a plant is exposed during the whole course of its existence to two opposing forces in connection with the general and the chlorophyllian respiration, the one tending to add and the other to abstract the material; and that according to the relation between these two forces, governed, as they are, by the intensity of light and of temperature, a plant will emit either oxygen or carbonic acid in variable proportions. In a feebly illuminated locality a plant remains in some sort stationary during whole months; and in absolute darkness, the eliminatory force being the only one in existence, the plant can only live upon its own resources, emit carbonic acid by combustion of these, and finally perish without increase of weight.

Further, and which is more expressly to my purpose, M. Boussingault says that " at certain epochs, in certain organs, the plant becomes, like an animal, an apparatus of combustion,—it burns carbon and hydrogen, it produces heat," and " a plant grown in darkness really behaves like (*se comporte comme*) an animal during the whole duration of its existence." An animal of the most simple organization not only produces heat through respiration, and emits carbonic acid, but a certain portion of the albumen which it contains is modified by the respiratory combustion into a crystalline, nitrogenized compound (*urea*). In the respiratory combustion of a plant growing in darkness, a like modification of the albumen could scarcely be as palpable, from the want of excretory organs; but we find in the juice filling the cells a crystalline immediate principle (*asparagine*), which, like the other, is an *amide*, becoming as easily transformed into aspartate of ammonia, as the former into carbonate of ammonia.

Thus the asparagus plants,† whilst flourishing in the light of the sun, produce no *asparagine*, but this is formed as a result of the *general respiration* when the light is excluded. It is easy to see how strongly these experiments confirm the results of the exclusion of light in the process of mossing adopted by Mr. M'Ivor. It is remarkable that green light is nearly the same in its effect as darkness, so that the shade of trees producing this coloured light is unfavourable to the development of vegetation. On the other hand, the products of the etiolated vegetation must be better adapted to sustain the life of those insects which always attack, in preference, plants of enfeebled organization.

The Woody Fibre of the Bark.

In order to complete my review of the question whereabouts in the bark the alkaloids are situated, and to put the reader in some measure in possession of the views of others on the subject, I will subjoin‡ a translation of a paper on this special subject by Dr. Flückiger, of Berne, presenting, as I think, the most recent, as well as the most correct views of the subject. It will be seen that the opinions of this talented observer are fully in accordance with those which I have expressed; and, as it seems to me, that he has, by well-devised experiments, shown that the views of Schacht and Wigand are not capable of being sustained.

I here present to the reader the results of some experiments of my own, tending to show more fully, and in different barks, the actual contents in alkaloid of the liber and of the cellular envelope.

Experiments.

The following experiments were instituted with a view of further comparison of the contents of the liber and of the cellular envelope. The plan adopted was the same that I have previously described. A

---

* " De la végétation dans l'obscurité" (Ann. de Chimie et de Physique, Fév. 1868).
† And others capable of producing asparagine; the same holds good as to solanine from the potato.
‡ In the Appendix.

large, thick piece of each sort was chosen, and carefully divided into two portions of equal weight, one of the inner, the other of the outer bark. Of each of these, 1000 grains were then taken and subjected to analysis :—

No. 1.—C. SUCCIRUBRA (Pavon).

Thickness of bark, average ½ inch.

Inside.			Outside.		
*Quinine, cryst. as oxalate	.	0·50	*Quinine, cryst. as sulphate	.	3·36
Do. uncryst.	. . .	1·90	Do. cryst. as oxalate	.	2·24
		—— 2·40	Do. uncryst.	. . .	2·20
					—— 7·80
Cinchonidine, hydriodate	. .	1·20	Cinchonidine, hydriodate	.	0·70
Cinchonine	. . . .	0·56	cryst. from other	.	1·20
Cinchonicine	. . . .	0·13			—— 1·90
		——	Cinchonine	. .	. 0·76
		4·29	Cinchonicine	. .	. 0·20
					——
					10·66

No. 2.—SPURIOUS RED BARK.

Thickness, ⅜ inch; inside especially woody.

Inside.			Outside.		
Cinchonidine	. . . .	0·50	*Sulph. Cinchonidine .	.	0·60
Cinchonine	. . . .	0·27	Cinchonine	.	0·30
		——			——
		0·77			0·90

No. 3.—C. ALMAGUERENSIS.

Approaches in appearance to Red bark, with leaves like *C. Pitayensis*. Thickness, ½ to ⅜ inch.

Inside.			Outside.		
Oxalate of Quinine	. . .	0·40	Oxalate of Quinine	. . .	1·00
Quinidine, with trace of Cincho-			Cinchonidine, and trace of Quini-		
nidine	. . . .	0·68	dine	. . . .	0·60
Cinchonine	. . . .	0·35	Cinchonine	. . .	0·25
Cinchonicine	. . . .	0·05	Cinchonicine	. . . .	0·75
		——			——
		1·48			2·00

No. 4.—C. PALTON.

Saffron-coloured bark, very fibrous internally. Thickness, ⅜ inch.

Inside.			Outside.		
Sulph. Quinine	.	0·85	Quinine, sulph.	.	1·83
Do. uncryst.	. .	0·47	Do. uncryst.	. .	0·80
		—— 1·32			—— 2·63
Cinchonicine	.	. 0·04	Cinchonicine	. . . .	0·04
		——			——
		1·36			2·67

No. 5.—C. LANCIFOLIA. Var. 7.

Great contrast between the fibrous inner bark and the cellular envelope. Thickness, 1/16 inch.

Inside.			Outside.		
Quinine, sulphate	. . .	0·60	Quinine, sulphate	.	1·80
Cinchonidine	. . . .	0·40	Cinchonidine	.	0·50
Cinchonicine	. . . .	0·15	Cinchonicine		0·15
		——			——
		1·15			2·45

---

* In order to secure *minute* accuracy, the weight of the sulphuric or of the oxalic acid should be deducted from the salts in combination (as the reader will find in my Table, p. 17). *Practically*, I find more instruction from the statement of results *as obtained*.

No. 6.—C. LUCUMÆFOLIA, Pav.

Very thick, woody bark, coarse fibre internally.   Thickness, ¾ to ⅝ inch.

Inside.			Outside.		
Quinine, sulphate	.	0·85	Quinine, sulphate	.	1·37
Do. uncryst.	.	0·05	Do. uncryst.	.	0·20
		—— 0·90			—— 1·57
Cinchonicine	.	0·80	Cinchonicine	.	0·85
		1·70			2·42

Mr. Broughton writes me (under date March 16th, 1868), "I have just repeated a capital experiment of yours, that of separating the liber from the external cortical portion deprived of periderm of the bark. The yield in Quinine in the former and latter was nearly as 3 to 5. As the 'Bastzellen' increase with age, the already marked difference will doubtless be augmented. The above has been made with great care, and checked by crystallization and a stoichiometrical trial."

To prove in another method the chemical composition, especially of the liber-fibres, I subjected the inner and outer bark (as above) of the *C. succirubra* to the following comparative examination :—

	Inner, per cent.	Outer, per cent.
Soluble in caustic liquor	13	23
Soluble in dilute hydrochloric acid	43	37
Soluble in chlorine water*	..	..
Soluble in nitric acid; soluble in sulphuric acid with subsequent black coloration, and separation of carbon by addition of water .	44	40†

I have in former publications fully expressed my own opinion on the subject, and I may here be permitted to add that continued observation and investigation have confirmed in my mind the views I have all along expressed, and that it is gratifying to find these confirmed by Dr. Flückiger and Mr. Broughton. Mr. Broughton (letter, December 9, 1867) says, "I have quite come to your conclusion, that the woody part of the liber is *adverse to* the existence of much alkaloid. Indeed, I believe I even extend your opinion."

My difference with the great German authorities, Schacht and Wigand, as to the woody fibre being, in their views of the subject, the seat of the alkaloids, was not of my seeking; and since I became acquainted, not without some surprise, with the views entertained by them, I have gone over the ground again with some care, and with much additional confirmation of the views I continue to hold. It is to me more than ever evident that it would be as wise for a butcher to select cattle having the largest amount of bone in proportion to their flesh as the most fitted for the tables of his customers, as to reckon upon the woody fibre as available for the extraction of Quinine, when the woody fibres themselves, as dissolved by chemical means, do not afford the hope of any different constitution from woody fibre of ordinary composition; and would not even serve for as much in the manufacture of Quinine as the dried bones of cattle would for the purposes of general nutrition.

There remains, of course, the question whether the spiral concavity in the centre of the fibres might not have been filled with combinations of the alkaloid, or whether the cell-walls might not have been impregnated with the same, as they doubtless are, at times, with colouring-matter.‡ It seems to me that a simple rule of proportion would soon settle this question. If the reader will observe the proportion which the liber fibres bear to the rich, renewed bark in Plate II., Figs. 1, 2, and 3, he will find it impossible to imagine that one-tenth part of the whole contents of the bark in the shape of alkaloids can have been lodged in so small a space.

Finally, and, as it appears to me, conclusively, the liber fibres, after having been subjected to the

---

* Gives a yellow colour for the *inner*, an orange colour for the *outer*, by addition of ammonia : no appreciable loss of weight.
† Less slight residuum.   ‡ *Vide* Illustr. Nueva Quin.

action of weak caustic liquor, then of dilute acid, present when acted on with chlorine water, the characteristics of *ligneous cuticle* of MM. Fremy and Terreil,[*] leaving a residuum which dissolves and blackens in sulphuric acid, and which is, I suppose, the *incrusting substance* of M. Payen, not showing a trace of alkaloid. How, then, can these fibres be the seat of the alkaloids?

Crystals from the Sap.

I have said that the sap is peculiar, but I do not find in cutting across the stem of young plants of the species any visible appearance in the abundant sap to distinguish it at first from the juice of other plants. It so happens, however, that in the *dried* barks rich in alkaloids which I examine, I find salts generally, if not always, in a state of granulation, or I might even say, of such crystallization as is to be expected from the *kinates* of these alkaloids, which, as is well known, are of a very soluble nature. This appearance, as seen under the microscope, is shown in the third Plate of the present volume. In the Red bark we find the *kinovates* much more abundant; also the occurrence of those very marked and peculiar crystals which are represented in my first Plates, and which I have before abundantly described. I have no thought that any deduction can be drawn from them other than that which I have given, and certainly not that any practical conclusion can thence be deduced as to the goodness of the bark.

My German friends naturally enough inquire how it is that they cannot find crystals which I see, and which our most skilful English draughtsmen find no difficulty in delineating. I have had the pleasure of showing those who have visited me the whole of my process, and convincing them by ocular demonstration that these crystals exist. The mode I employ in preparing the section of the bark, is to boil it for a few seconds in a very weak caustic solution, then to wash in abundance of water, and place the slice at once under the microscope,—the whole not occupying five minutes,—so that it is chemically impossible that any crystals (especially of quite soluble salts) could be formed under the circumstances. I call these crystals *quite soluble* (though far less soluble than the kinates I have mentioned), since they gradually dissolve, and in the course of a few weeks disappear in any menstruum that I know how to employ,—in this respect showing the difference of their nature from that of raphides or the granulations of inorganic salts in the crystal cells of the same bark, as also from the starch granules which are sometimes met with.

I do not profess that my plan is so elaborate as theirs,—it simply presents the natural appearances with less alteration; and it was not till after long disappointment with preparations made in the manner ordinarily practised in England that I adopted the present more simple arrangement.

Isolated Vessels.

Whilst subjecting the very rich renewed bark of *C. succirubra* to microscopical examination, I met with a curious exemplification of the production of isolated reticulate vessels in a part of the plant where they have been rarely (if at all) observed in the same position, viz. in the bark itself. I had the opportunity of hearing a very interesting paper by Herbert Spencer, Esq., read before the Linnean Society, since published in the Transactions of this body in 1866, which enters into the question of the function of these spiral cells, and is accompanied by well-executed drawings resembling entirely those which I now present to the reader. The author reconsiders the question whether such vessels ought not to be looked upon as carriers of the plant juices, and adduces satisfactory evidence, as I think, to prove the affirmative of this proposition. Such vessels are found in leaves, and in the young and succulent parts of plants, also, as shown by Trécul, in some renewed tissues, but not ordinarily in the bark of trees. Their occurrence, as

---

[*] 'Journal de Pharmacie et de Chimie,' Avril 1868.

presented in my Plates, seems to imply, in this instance, an abnormal state in the newly renewed bark, the source and tendency of which is not at first apparent. Though I made perhaps twenty sections of the one bundle observed, I failed to find these in other portions, but have again met with similar vessels in a recent remittance of the third harvest of renewed bark. In the plates accompanying M. Trécul's observations are seen the adventitious roots produced by a *Gleditschia* and by an *Ulmus*, in consequence of decortication,—showing what might perhaps be called an effort of the plant to regain its normal state and the needful channel for its descending sap; and the vessels I have figured may be a tendency to the production of adventitious roots or buds, such as are figured in connection with the paper of the above botanist, where the important part assigned to these vessels is clearly seen, and their occasional isolation mentioned as having been observed by the author.[*]

The Laticiferous Ducts.

I have hitherto taken little notice of the laticiferous ducts, and yet these must play a not unimportant, however obscure, part in the economy of the plant. The latex is one of the products which approach the most nearly to those of the animal creation, and it has been compared with the blood; but in my opinion it has more analogy with the biliary secretion, inasmuch as it is a secretion, and not the very life of the plant, which latter the blood seems to be in a certain sense to animals, and the chlorophyll to plants, and also to some animalcules.

It may not improbably differ from the surrounding cell-formation in its electro-chemical state, and may perform important services to the young developing structures, since it appears to be connected with quickening and stimulating them; and in the researches of M. Decaisne it was noticed by him that those portions of the cellular structure of the madder through which these ducts permeated were the first to change colour from yellow to red, as though by the addition of oxygen gas. I have also noticed that these ducts are the first portions of the structure to manifest the alteration when a deterioration takes place in the health of the plant. The latex, under these circumstances, changes colour, and gradually turns black. But in what relation are we to conceive of these ducts as standing towards the formation of the alkaloids?

In the first place, it is certain that, in proportion as the alkaloids become more abundantly developed, the laticiferous ducts disappear, as in the fully matured flat *Calisaya* bark, or else become much restricted in their size and relative extent and importance, as in the Red bark; in which last again the persistence to a certain extent of these ducts may be connected with a more abundant development of kinovic acid in the *C. succirubra* than is present in most other barks.

In the next place, where they do not disappear, as in some inferior barks, such as the *C. ovata*, an inferior production of alkaloid occurs, and of this poverty there is no more certain sign than the occurrence of wide, open, laticiferous vessels; further, that in the allied genus of *Ladenbergia* (or *Cascarilla*), in which these assume large proportions and are permanent, it is kinova-bitter alone that is predominant. Large development of these ducts, therefore, indicates large production of kinova-bitter, and diminishing and disappearing laticiferous vessels indicate abundant formation of alkaloid.

The conclusion, therefore, to which I arrive is, that laticiferous ducts exist for the secretion of kinova-bitter,—at least in the present families of plants under review. On the other hand, their disappearance is connected with the change of the kinova-bitter or its elements into alkaloid; and that not in these ducts, but rather in the parenchymatous cell formation.

---

[*] " Sur l'origine des bourgeons adventifs" (Ann. des Sc. Nat., tome viii. 1847). " Dans les bourgeons adventifs, ce sont des *vaisseaux réticulés qui deviennent ponctués*, qui se montrent d'abord." (Ann. des Sc., tome xvii., ibid. p. 268; see also tome viii. 1847, p. 290.) " J'ai vu aussi quelquefois des vaisseaux isolés, non accompagnés des tissus qui entourent ordinairement ces organes, répandues au milieu des fibres du liber." (Ibid. tome viii. 1847.)

I have previously copied[*] from Dr. De Vrij a table showing the relative proportion of kinova-bitter in the different parts of the *Calisaya*, and I may here add a more recent observation of the same chemist, that the leaves of *C. succirubra* grown at the low elevation of Peradenia (1600 feet above the sea) contained twice as much kinova-bitter as leaves of the same grown at Ootacamund (7416 feet), preserving still the same inverse ratio to the proportion of alkaloids which pervades the whole structure of the plant.

The Mother-substance of the Cinchona.

This substance is found only in the wood; it does not coexist with the Cinchona-red, and but in a very minor proportion with the alkaloids, but on its breaking up into Cinchona-red the formation of the alkaloids seems in some way to depend. It is then, at all events, worthy of close investigation.

The Cinchona-red is produced by a process of slow oxidation in the bark of the plant. This process, as I have shown, is very gradual, and is by no means complete when the dried bark comes into the hands of the chemist. It must be remembered that this change does not commence in the wood, which retains its yellowish hue unchanged, but the bark assumes either a reddish[†] appearance (as in the species we are considering), or more or less tawny, if the Cinchona-red is masked by other principles. This Cinchona-red is found in all the valuable Cinchonæ, although in part replaced in the aricine-producing plants by a kindred substance of intensely orange colour.

The process which I found most advantageous to extract the colouring matter from the wood was to dissolve it out by ether, which, as a neutral substance, seemed incapable of exercising any influence on its chemical composition, and was consequently best adapted to give it into my hands in a state of purity, and, as far as first appearances went, of homogeneous composition. On evaporating the dissolving medium, the substance was left in appearance resinous, brittle, almost inodorous, and perfectly stable in its composition under all circumstances. It does not attract moisture nor absorb oxygen from the air, and thus differs sensibly from the Cinchotannic acid found by Schwartz in the *Calisaya* bark, and which he rightly described[‡] as passing rapidly under the influence of ammonia and of the oxygen of the air into Cinchona-red. The present substance must nevertheless stand in very near relation to that of Schwartz, but also in equally near relation to another substance which he derived from the same bark, and which he calls Chinovic acid.[§] Schwartz considered this to be identical with a substance (Quinovin) previously found by Hlasiwetz[||] in the *Quina nova*.

The proof of the near relationship existing in this Mother-substance to both Cinchona-red and Kinovic acid is found, first in the action of alkalies, metallic oxides, or alkaloids, which produce the red colour by their action on the mother-substance. Thus the addition of ammonia to the light yellow ethereal solution gives rise at once to a fine rose-colour; and when all is evaporated down together, there remains a compound of kinovic acid and ammonia coloured by Cinchona-red, which appears as an excretory product. The powerful alkalies break up the substance in this manner at once, but the operation of earths and metallic oxides is more slow. Thus, when a piece of lime is dropped into the ethereal solution and allowed to stand in the sunlight, which seems to favour the process, the Cinchona-red is very gradually deposited on the lime, which assumes nearly the appearance of red coral; and in this case nearly the whole of the Mother-substance seems to pass in time into Cinchona-red, and it thus appears to contain *the elements* of cinchotannic acid; but when lime-water is made to act upon the same substance, it dissolves this with the

* Illustr. Nueva Quinologia, *sub voce C. magnifolia*.
† The appearance is *exactly* described by the Spanish name of the best Red Bark, *la teja, i.e.* resembling *a tile*; another kind, equally abundant, of a different aspect, which I have described, is called *la morada*, with equal propriety. This latter, according to Mr. R. Cross, who gives me the above information, is of a different species to the *C. succirubra* (? *C. conglomerata*).
‡ 'Annalen der Chemie und Pharmacie,' lxxx. p. 332.   § 'Centralblatt,' 1852, p. 194.
|| Ann. der Chemie und Pharm. lxxiv. p. 138.

manifestation of a pink colour, which, combining with excess of lime, forms a pink lake. When the filtered solution is precipitated by hydrochloric acid, a separation of Kinova-bitter takes place, with its usual appearance, and apparently almost milk-white. When this is collected, however, and again acted on by lime, a pink lake, but of a fainter hue, is again formed, and so on for several repetitions before the product which I have mentioned is obtained pure, and free from colour.

I wish it to be understood that I do not assert the *homogeneity* of this mother-substance, nor suppose that it can be recognized as *a chemically pure body*, but I like to follow Nature in her operations, and to study the *becoming* as well as the *being* of her products.

The pure kinovic acid is easily obtained from kinova-bitter. If the Mother-substance is mixed with an ethereal solution of Quinine, a combination takes place which I have described as Kinovate of Quinine, and have represented the crystals it forms.* From this combination there seems to be a slow separation of Cinchona-red, as happens with lime above. I have no doubt that this is the state of combination in which the alkaloids exist, more especially in the Red Bark. It is this which explains the reason why aqueous infusions of Red Bark are deficient in strength, which is not so much the case when they are made from barks in which the alkaloids are united to kinic acid. It is, moreover, as I have before explained, chiefly this curious state of combination which renders the extraction of the alkaloids a matter of so much difficulty. The attempt to manufacture sulphate of Quinine on the spot where the trees are found has always failed (though often attempted in South America), and equally profitless has been the attempt to precipitate the alkaloids and send them over mixed with lime;—in this last case also other deteriorating effects were produced. Spirituous tinctures dissolve more of the alkaloids, but also of partially oxidized Cinchona-red, which gradually separates by slow oxidation.

The Mother-substance of the Cascarilla.

I am indebted to Señor Pedro Rada for specimens of the *Mula Cascarilla* or *Cascarilla Carua* of Weddell, consisting of leafy branches with very fine leaves of some 18 inches long, and also of sections of branches covered with bark. I was thus enabled to examine the wood in reference to its constituents as compared with that of the Cinchona. A peculiar colouring matter is very abundant in this Cascarilla, so as to form *apparently* a dark purple or almost black incrustation on the external portion of the bark. It is, therefore, to be expected that some analogous mother-substance should exist in the wood. This I found to be the case, for in treating the wood, rasped to a fine powder, with ether, and evaporating, I obtained a lemon-coloured, resinous-looking substance, similar in some of its properties to that of the Cinchona. The ethereal solution, treated with lime, gave a deposit of what might be called *Cascarilla-red*, and, when shaken up with caustic or with liquor ammoniæ, a fine, rich, characteristic colour was developed in the solution, and the supernatant ethereal solution became partly filled with crystals, the precise nature of which I could not determine. On the whole, the great contrast between the colouring matter in these allied genera seems to be that in the Cinchona the mother-substance is *very slowly* oxidized in connection with the formation of the alkaloids; but in the Cascarilla the process is more rapid, and perhaps more complete.

When the wood is treated with milk of lime, a considerable amount of kinova-bitter is obtained by the addition of acid to the filtered solution.

Products of the Cells.

It will be observed that none of the substances I have noticed are nitrogenized bodies nor capable of acting powerfully on the human frame. The additional step to the formation of alkaloid from these, I suppose to be taken in the cells of the bark, commencing more especially with the cambium. I have

---

* 'Microscopical Observations,' pl. ii. fig. 12 b.

sought to add the nitrogenous element to the mother-substance by means of heating a solution of it, together with chloride of ammonium, in a sealed tube, for twenty-four hours, at a temperature of 200° Fahrenheit, but found it entirely unchanged. Other tentative processes have not as yet proved more successful. I regret being unable to follow the curious chemistry of the parenchymatous cells of the liber and of the cellular envelope, but must refer to what I have before written* to show that the flow of the nourishing sap not only conveys to these the substances on which this chemical transformation is effected, but that also these products can be removed by the same circulation when the need of other parts requires, and the whole then becomes changed into the outside corky layer.

The hot and dry air arising from the valleys of the Patia, was believed by Karsten to have been the cause of the inferior production of alkaloid in the trees of *C. lancifolia* growing on the volcano of Pasto.† This might well be the case if the material was *used up* by the plant for its necessities thus created; as, in other cases, the provision of starch is consumed by the plant in flowering.

The alkaloids must be regarded as highly complex, and, so to speak, animalized products of the *general* respiration,‡ being in this way fitted to act powerfully on the animal economy (the blood having an alkaline reaction); as conversely acid gases of simple constitution (sulphurous, nitrous, etc.) are deadly poison to vegetables whose juice has an acid reaction.

In studying the effect of the processes of chemical action continually going forward in the cells, I am obliged to feel the insufficiency of our skill and the incompleteness of our present appliances for investigating the secrets of this wondrous laboratory of nature.

The determination of the constituent elements of organized structure by what we call analysis, must pass for what it is worth and no more. When we have dried all the molecules of water out of an egg, and then subject the remainder to analysis, we examine simply a spoiled product, differing so widely from the original that it can by no means be brought again into its primitive state, and all the remarkable capacities connected with its primitive organization are at an end. It is not different when we examine the vegetable cell; with the utmost care and delicacy of research, the most important points still remain unexplained. The microscope reveals to sight much which chemical analysis cannot follow.

Latest Remittance from the East Indies.

In the month of August of the present year, 1868, I received the eighth remittance of specimens from Ootacamund, and have sent a Report thereon to the Indian Government, which the reader will find reprinted in the Appendix.

I gather several points of instruction from the examination of these specimens :—

1. The permanence of the characteristics of species,§ as far as ascertained by the present investigation. After all the changes and the varied treatment of the *Cinchona succirubra*, it appears to remain exactly the same in all material points as in South America.

2. It appears that the renewed bark must derive its peculiarities from the nourishing sap, and not from the leaves, since the one-year-old renewed bark partakes of the five-years-old characteristics of the plant on which it grows.

3. The implication of the resinous principle with the alkaloids increases with age in the *C. succirubra*, and thus produces increased difficulty in their extraction.

4. On this account the Red Bark Tree should not be relied upon as forming the chief element in any plantation.

---

* 'Microscopical Observations,' pl. ii. fig. 12 *b*, p. 2.   † 'The Chinchona Species of New Granada,' p. 97.
‡ Analogous to *Kreatin* and *Neurin* in the animal economy.   § See also under D. in the Appendix.

I

5. The cells of the root-bark seem to have a peculiar aptitude for the formation of Cinchonine, agreeing in this respect with the cells of bark grown under dense shade.

6. Cultivation of the Red Bark Tree for the sake of the roots would not answer as a commercial speculation, unless, from altered circumstances, Cinchonine were in greater demand than it is at present.

Conclusion.

In conclusion, I must resume some of the leading points, which appear to be shown with more or less clearness.

1. That the cultivation of the Cinchonæ in India promises complete success, but to ensure this, great attention must be paid to the choice of species.

2. That if properly conducted it will prove remunerative.

3. That Mr. M'Ivor's plan of mossing is an important discovery in the direction of intelligent culture.

4. That the renewal of the bark from the cambium leads to different conclusions as to the permanence of the supply of fresh bark, from those to be deduced from the theory of formation of the alkaloids in the leaves.

5. That no part of the tree—root, stem, or leaves—visited by the ascending sap, seems to be the place of deposit of the alkaloids.

6. That these are formed in the cellular tissue of the bark, beginning from the cambium outwards.

7. That the sources whence the materials are drawn for this elaboration are at once the nourishing sap descending in its usual course, and a lateral conveyance, through the medullary rays, of part of the deposit of the mother-substance in the wood.

8. That inasmuch as this mother-substance is characteristic of the Cinchonæ, and is the source of the Cinchona-red, it may also mainly conduce to the formation of the alkaloids, since it is probable that the characteristic principle of each plant is originally *one*.

9. That the above principle, deduced by M. Decaisne from his researches on Madder, is equally true as to Red bark.

10. That no explanation is at present offered of the tendency of the cells in the root of the Madder to secrete the peculiar colouring-matter, nor in the bark of the Cinchonæ to produce alkaloid.

11. That the electro-chemical properties of the cells are nevertheless greatly influenced by the respiration, and that by changing the character of this respiration we may artificially control their action.

12. That the *chlorophyllian* respiration does not favour, but that the *general* respiration does favour the production of alkaloids.

13. That the presence or absence of light has great influence (through the respiration) on all the above phenomena.

14. That the laticiferous ducts dwindle and disappear coincidently with the formation of the alkaloids.

15. That the liber fibres are not the place of deposit of the alkaloids.

16. That in the liber the alkaloids are found in the state of the greatest purity, but in the outside cellular tissue these are more abundantly stored up; especially this is the case as to Quinine.

Tottenham, 1868.

APPENDIX.

A. (Page 5.)—Address of Dr. Weddell to the Botanical Congress (1867) in Paris.

Sur la Culture des Quinquinas. Par M. H.-A. Weddell.

Messieurs,—C'est avec une vive satisfaction que je me vois chargé, par mon ami M. J.-Eliot Howard, de Londres, d'appeler l'attention du Congrès sur les échantillons que j'ai l'honneur de déposer sur le bureau. Cette satisfaction, vous la comprendrez et vous la partagerez, je crois, lorsque vous saurez que les écorces mises sous vos yeux ont été retirées de caisses débarquées, il y a quelques jours, sur les quais de Londres, et renfermant la première récolte que les plantations de *Cinchona* de l'Inde anglaise aient livrée au commerce européen. Ces écorces témoignent donc du succès d'une entreprise qui, au point de vue de l'humanité, peut être regardée à juste titre comme une des plus utiles de notre siècle.

Les progrès de la culture des *Cinchona*, dans les Indes, ont été exposés dans plusieurs ouvrages de date assez récente. Je demande néanmoins la permission d'eu dire ici quelques mots ici, j'ose l'espérer, ne seront pas sans intérêt, surtout en vue des pièces qui vous sont soumises. Et puisque ces pièces me rappellent encore tout naturellement le nom de M. Howard, je dirai, en commençant, que, par ses profondes connaissances en quinologie, aussi bien que par son habileté comme chimiste, et par son noble désintéressement, notre éminent confrère a rendu à cette œuvre les plus importants services, et doit être mis au premier rang de ceux qui ont contribué à sa réussite. A la science, il en a rendu de non moins grands;* mais je me contenterai, en ce moment, de rappeler que c'est en grande partie à son tact persévérant que l'on a dû de connaître enfin l'origine botanique du vrai Quinquina rouge, dont vous avez précisément ici les écorces sous les yeux.

La première tentative de culture des *Cinchona*, dans les Indes britanniques, eut lieu en 1853,† époque à laquelle un certain nombre de plants de *C. Calisaya*, d'origine française, y furent transportés sous la surveillance de M. Fortune. Ce ne fut cependant que quelques années après, en 1859, que le gouvernement anglais se mit sérieusement à l'œuvre, en envoyant au Pérou M. Clements Markham. Ce voyageur, auquel on doit les plus grands éloges pour le zèle et la persévérance qu'il a déployés dans la mission difficile qui lui était confiée, partit d'Angleterre avec un habile jardinier (M. Weir), aborda au Pérou, par le port de Callao, et se dirigea ensuite sur celui d'Islay, pour gagner la province de Carabaya, où il suivit, à peu de chose près, l'itinéraire que j'y avais suivi moi-même, une douzaine d'années auparavant. Il y recueillit, non sans difficulté, un grand nombre de plants de *Cinchona* qui furent confiés à des caisses de Ward, mais qui moururent malheureusement tous pendant la traversée, on peu après leur arrivée à Madras; perte considérable, mais qui ne fit pas, fort heureusement, péricliter l'entreprise elle-même. En effet, M. Markham n'avait pas voulu en confier le succès à ses souls moyens. Dès avant son départ d'Angleterre, il avait eu soin d'enrôler au profit de l'œuvre quelques hommes aussi habiles que dévoués, parmi lesquels on doit citer en première ligne le botaniste Spruce,‡ auquel on dut d'obtenir bientôt de jeunes plants, et surtout des graines, de plusieurs espèces de *Cinchona*, dont l'expérience avait depuis longtemps démontré la valeur. La perte de la récolte de M. Markham se trouva ainsi amplement compensée.

Quelques-unes des graines obtenues de la sorte furent semées dans les serres du Jardin royal do Kew,§ en Angleterre; les autres, dirigées immédiatement sur l'Inde, y furent distribuées entre divers sites signalés comme étant les plus propres à fournir aux plantes à cultiver les conditions de sol et de climat qu'elles trouvent dans leur pays natal. Il est inutile de suivre les péripéties de cette culture dans ces diverses localités; bornons-nous à l'étudier dans celle qui a produit les échantillons que nous avons devant nous, c'est-à-dire, Ootacamund, dans les montagnes de Nilghiri. Cette plantation, placée sous la direction de M. M'Ivor, ne tarda pas, grâce à la rare intelligence de ce cultivateur, à atteindre un degré de prospérité qui doit nécessairement la faire prendre pour modèle de toutes celles qu'on pourra établir par la suite. Quelques chiffres montreront du reste, beaucoup mieux que toute description, les rapides progrès de l'établissement. Ainsi, quand M. M'Ivor s'établit à Ootacamund, en mars 1861, il y rencontra 685 plants de *Cinchona*, la plupart appartenant au *C. succirubra*. Eh bien! en avril 1862, il y en avait 31,495, et, un an après, 157,704. Le dernier recensement avait eu lieu en avril 1863. Au mois de décembre de cette même année, le nombre des plants de *Cinchona* existant à Ootacamund était de 277,080! A partir de ce moment, on ne les compte, pour ainsi dire, plus; et, à l'heure qu'il est, c'est presque par millions qu'on peut les dénombrer. Dans la seule propriété particulière de Dova

---

* Le magnifique ouvrage publié par M. Howard sous le titre de 'Illustrations of the Nueva Quinologia of Pavon' (1 vol. in-fol. avec 30 planches coloriées) est connu de tout le monde.

† Le premier pas officiel fait ou Angleterre pour introduire la culture des *Cinchona* dans les Indes britanniques l'a été à la suite d'une dépêche du gouverneur-général de l'Inde, en date du 27 mars 1852.

‡ C'est par le zèle infatigable de M. Spruce que le gouvernement a *été* mis en possession du *C. succirubra*, qui rivalise avec le *C. Calisaya* par l'importance de ses produits, et d'autres espèces du versant occidental des Indes de l'Équateur. M. Cross accompagnait M. Spruce, comme jardinier, dans cette expédition, et fit ensuite, seul, deux autres voyages quinologiques, avec le même succès: l'un au district de Loxa, l'autre à Pitayo, dans la Nouvelle Grenade. M. Pritchett visitait pendant ce temps les montagnes d'Huanuco, et recueillait ces graines et de jeunes plants des espèces de cette localité classique.—Voyez, pour d'amples détails sur ce sujet, le très-intéressant volume de M. Markham, intitulé, 'Travels in Peru and India.'

§ Alors sous la direction du célèbre Sir William Hooker, lequel n'a jamais cessé, non plus que son illustre fils, le directeur actuel, d'apporter le plus vif intérêt à toutes les questions qui se rattachent à la culture des Quinquinas.

Shola, il y en a 900,000; et l'enthousiasme pour cette culture est tel, qu'indigènes et étrangers, rajas et paysans, tous veulent avoir leur plantation de Quinquinas. J'ajoute que cette immense multiplication a été obtenue par un système de bouturage par très-petits tronçons, grâce auquel, par exemple, un pied de *C. officinalis Uritusinga*, présenté au gouvernement par M. Howard, et arrivé dans l'Inde en avril 1862, a pu compter, dix-neuf mois après, 6850 rejetons.

Les résultats que je viens de faire connaître sont déjà bien remarquables, mais ceux dont il me reste à parler tiennent presque du prodige.

Aux débuts de cette grande expérience, c'est-à-dire, il y a quinze ans, on pouvait craindre que le rendement des écorces ne diminuât, par suite de la culture de l'arbre dans des conditions qui ne seraient pas tout à fait celles où il végète en Amérique; tout au moins devait-on avoir quelques doutes sur le résultat; eh bien! on est en droit aujourd'hui d'affirmer que la richesse des écorces de *Cinchona* cultivés dans l'Inde, sera non-seulement égale à celle des écorces américaines, mais arrivera même peut-être, dans certains cas, à être double et peut-être plus considérable encore. Ceci n'est pas aujourd'hui une hypothèse, mais un fait; et M. M'Ivor a obtenu ce résultat par un moyen si simple que je n'exagérais pas en disant que les résultats obtenus tenaient presque du prodige. Pour y arriver, il lui a suffi, en effet, d'appliquer sur l'écorce de l'arbre une couche de mousse qui la garantit, pendant une certaine période de sa croissance, de l'influence combinée de l'air et de la lumière. Ainsi, voici par exemple une écorce de *C. succirubra* développée à l'air libre et âgée de quatre ans; son rendement en alcaloïdes est de 0·95 pour 100. Si, au contraire, six mois seulement avant de l'enlever, vous l'eussiez enveloppé d'une couche de mousse, ce rendement aurait dépassé 9 pour 100. Ce n'est pas tout. Ce que cette application de mousse, ce que ce *moussage* de l'écorce offre peut-être de plus intéressant à noter, c'est qu'il permet à l'oubier d'un arbre dénudé de sa écorce, pour les besoins du commerce, d'en reproduire une seconde et même une troisième;* chacune de celles-ci étant non-seulement plus riche en alcaloïdes que l'écorce qui l'a précédée, mais étant proportionnellement plus riche en quinine, cette quinine étant en outre d'une extraction plus facile. Anatomiquement ces écorces diffèrent des autres par l'absence plus ou moins complète des fibres du liber. Enfin, un dernier fait qu'il faut signaler, parce qu'il peut résulter de la culture et qu'il pourra avoir une certaine importance quand on saura exactement sous quelles influences il se produit, c'est la conversion des alcaloïdes voisins l'un dans l'autre:† de la quinine, par exemple, en cinchonidine, ainsi que cela s'est vu dans le *C. Calisaya*, ou de la cinchonine ou quinidine, comme M. Howard l'a constaté pour le *C. micrantha*.

Je termine ici ce que j'avais à dire sur la culture des Quinquinas dans l'Inde anglaise, et je demande la permission d'appeler, pendant quelques instants, votre attention d'un autre côté.

C'est à l'Angleterre, nous l'avons vu, que revient la gloire d'avoir offert au monde les premiers fruits de la grande entreprise dont je vous ai retracé quelques-unes des phases les plus intéressantes. Mais, ceci reconnu, il n'est que juste de revendiquer pour deux autres nations la part de mérite qui leur est due dans le développement de cette œuvre bienfaisante. Ces pays sont la France et la Hollande. Je commence par la France, et ici je vous prierai de m'excuser si je mets en avant mon propre nom. Peut-être ne le ferais-je pas si j'étais seul en fait dans le léger oubli dont je crois avoir à me plaindre, mais comme cet oubli porte surtout sur un établissement public, établissement auquel j'ai été fier d'appartenir, je crois qu'il est de mon devoir, ou ce moment, de défendre ses droits. Ce que je réclame pour la France, c'est le mérite d'avoir suscité le mouvement qui a eu pour résultat les diverses tentatives faites pour cultiver le Quinquina, et d'avoir fait le premier pas dans la voie féconde où l'ont suivie, pour la devancer bientôt, la Hollande d'abord, l'Angleterre ensuite. Pour ce qui est de moi personnellement, je désire simplement constater que, quelles qu'aient été les suggestions faites antérieurement, ce n'est, en réalité, qu'à la suite de la publication de ma 'Monographie des Quinquinas,' en 1849, et du rapport dont elle a été l'objet; ce n'est que sous l'impression du cri d'alarme que j'y ai jeté, que l'attention des gouvernements a été éveillée, et que les premiers pas utiles ont été faits pour opérer le transport de la production et du commerce des Quinquinas du nouveau monde à l'ancien. Voilà, Messieurs, la part que j'ai eue dans cette œuvre. Cette œuvre appartient au Muséum d'Histoire Naturelle ces bien certainement importante. Il est d'abord, ne dois-je pas dire que c'est comme voyageur-naturaliste de cet établissement que j'ai été à même d'étudier l'état des forêts de Quinquinas, et d'appeler l'attention sur la destruction qui en menaçait les espèces les plus précieuses? Ce sont ensuite les graines de *Cinchona*, recueillies et remises par moi au Muséum, qui, semées dans les serres de cet établissement, sous la surveillance de M. Houllet, y ont levé et ont donné les premiers plants de Quinquina que l'on ait vus vivants en Europe. Ce sont enfin ces plants qui ont servi aux premiers essais de culture qui aient été faits, soit en Afrique, soit en Asie. Dès leur apparition, on se préoccupa, en effet, des moyens de les transporter sous des climats que l'on pouvait supposer propices à leur développement, et les premiers qui soient sortis de France furent adressés, en 1849, à M. Hardy, directeur des pépinières des environs d'Alger, et furent livrés à la pleine terre, dans l'établissement du Hamma. C'est là le premier essai de culture du Quinquina, à l'air libre, qui ait été tenté hors de son pays natal. Il ne fut pas heureux, et l'on doit, par cette raison même, regretter plus vivement encore que le gouvernement français n'ait pas donné alors une attention plus sérieuse à une question d'une importance aussi manifeste, en prenant en main l'œuvre dont le Muséum avait eu l'initiative.

La Hollande commença ses essais vers le moment où la France suspendait les siens, en 1852, par conséquent environ sept années avant que l'Angleterre, profitant des fautes comme de l'expérience de ses devanciers, entrât sérieusement dans la même voie. Le gouvernement hollandais savait que le Muséum avait distribué dans le commerce français un certain nombre de pieds de *Cinchona Calisaya*, nés dans ses serres. Il s'en procura chez MM. Thibant et Keteléer, et les fit transporter à Java. Ce sont les premiers qui aient respiré l'air des Indes. Ils provenaient, on le voit, du Muséum d'Histoire Naturelle. J'ai dit aussi,

---

* Les habitants de Loxa réussissaient parfois à obtenir de leurs arbres une seconde récolte, mais par un procédé bien moins parfait. Ils enlevaient l'écorce d'un seul côté du tronc. Les livres de la bande corticale laissée en place s'étendaient alors peu à peu et finissaient par recourir, plus ou moins complètement, la portion d'aubier dénudée.—Voyez Howard, *l. c. sub C. Uritusinga*.

† La valeur commerciale des alcaloïdes des Quinquinas, et par suite celle des écorces dont on les extrait, dérive en grande partie de leur rendement thérapeutique. Or, il résulte des rapports publiés récemment par des commissions siégeant à Madras et à Bombay, et dont l'objet est de s'assurer expérimentalement, et sur une grande échelle, de l'importance thérapeutique relative des quatre alcaloïdes de Quinquina actuellement employés, que les sulfates de cinchonine, de cinchonidine et de quinidine sont beaucoup plus efficaces qu'on ne le suppose généralement. Il est donc présumable que cette décision va donner du prix à bon nombre d'écorces que l'on a cessé d'exploiter, depuis que la croyance s'est répandue que la quinine possède seule à un haut degré les qualités dont on est obligé aujourd'hui de reconnaître l'existence, et seulement à un degré un peu moindre, chez ces trois sœurs, et en particulier dans la quinidine.

plus haut, que le premier envoi fait par l'Angleterre dans ses grandes possessions asiatiques était d'origine française. Les plants qui le composaient provenaient de la même source que ceux qui se trouvaient déjà dans les Indes néerlandaises: du Muséum d'Histoire Naturelle.

La Hollande ne s'en tint pas là. Dans cette même année 1852, elle fit partir pour le Pérou le botaniste Hasskarl, avec mandat d'y recueillir des plants et des graines de *Cinchona* et de les accompagner à Java; ce qui fut fait; mais, soit par une raison, soit par une autre, les progrès des plantations furent très-lents; si bien que lorsque, trois ans après, la direction des cultures vint à être confiée à M. Junghuhn, celui-ci n'y trouva que 351 arbres en pleine croissance. A partir de cette époque, cependant, la multiplication prend des proportions considérables, et, sans une circonstance qui est réellement à déplorer, les plantations des Indes néerlandaises n'auraient aujourd'hui rien à envier à celles de l'Inde britannique. Séduit par la plus grande rusticité d'un *Cinchona* d'espèce douteuse, né de graines rapportées par M. Hasskarl, on se prit à le multiplier au détriment d'autres espèces plus délicates peut-être, mais dont l'utilité était démontrée, et l'on reconnut, trop tard, que la plante qui avait coûté tant de soins n'avait que peu ou point de valeur commerciale:* de sorte que, bien qu'il y ait en ce moment plus d'un million d'arbres à Quinquina dans l'île de Java, la proportion des bonnes espèces y est relativement faible. Je n'exagère donc pas beaucoup en disant que l'opération devra y être reprise presque en entier, en n'y employant, cette fois, que les espèces ou variétés† dont l'expérience, ou mieux encore, l'analyse chimique, aura démontré la valeur. C'est en procédant ainsi que l'Angleterre est arrivée, presque du premier coup, à la solution du problème.

B. (Page 6).—FIRST REPORT, ETC. (Extract).

From J. E. HOWARD, F.L.S., *to* C. R. MARKHAM, Esq. (May 28, 1863.)

"1. I have great pleasure in informing you that the result of my examination of the bark of *C. succirubra* grown in India is very satisfactory. I have, thus far, only operated upon 500 grains, proceeding cautiously, as the quantity of bark sent is small. I find exactly the same constituents as in South American 'Red Bark,' and was able to obtain a first and second crystallization of very white sulphate of quinine, mixed (as is usual when obtained from 'Red Bark') with sulphate of cinchonidine. I have also obtained some cinchonine.

"2. This must be considered a very satisfactory and promising result, when the immature age of the bark is considered (viz. two years' growth), and especially when I add that the percentage product of alkaloid appears to me as great as would be met with in South America under the same circumstances."

C. (Page 22.)

On the Anatomy of the Bark of Cinchonas. By F. A. FLÜCKIGER. ('Wochenschrift für Pharmacie,' Bern, No. 47, 48, Nov. 1866.)

The bark of the cinchona, as is well known, does not show any very striking anatomical peculiarity in contrast to other bark. The structure of the liber is the most distinctive feature. . . . The peculiarity consists in this, that the liber fibres, which are unusually short, begin to close up when still very young. The cellular wall is generally so thickened by layers on the inner side that the original hollow space is greatly decreased, and almost obliterated. These layers are so bound to each other and to the primary wall, that it is impossible to discern their exact arrangement. The best way to do so is to make a horizontal or oblique section. The beautiful colours which these thickened bast cells take in polarized light show that the cellular tissue is under strong tension.

The corresponding structure in other barks is either much longer, thinner, and more flexible, and not pointed at the end, or else with the hollow remaining, and therefore not so stiff as the bast cells of cinchona. The latter never ramify, whilst other liber cells, as, for instance, those of the so-called "false cinchona," divide and form a kind of network.

The question as to the situation of the alkaloids in the bark arose after Weddell's first investigations in 1849. "Flat *Calisaya*" was formerly considered as undeniably the most productive bark, and this yielded Weddell the largest number of liber fibres, and these most evenly distributed; wherefrom he concluded that these had some connection with the produce of quinine. He carried out this view by many very careful experiments, which cannot be set down here for fear of being too lengthy. Suffice it to say that he considered cinchonine to be chiefly contained in the outer layers and quinine in the inner ones. The amount of the latter corresponded, he thought, with the number of liber fibres only up to a certain point, and he considered the most fruitful structure to be that shown by the smooth *Calisaya*, namely, many short, isolated liber fibres, regularly and somewhat thickly placed in the parenchyma of the inner bark.

He pointedly contradicts‡ the view that the woody liber fibres themselves could contain an appreciable quantity of alkaloid.

---

* Ce *Cinchona*, provenant des environs d'Uchubamba, dans le Pérou central, a été reconnu nouveau par M. Howard, et a été dédié par lui au gouverneur-général des Indes néerlandaises, sous le nom de *C. Pahudiana.* L'espèce avait été confondue, paraît-il, antérieurement, avec le *C. ovata* et avec le *C. carabayensis*, dont elle est bien distincte. Des échantillons de l'écorce de cet arbre, ainsi que de celles de presque toutes les autres espèces de *Cinchona* cultivées jusqu'à ce jour dans les Indes, forment partie de la magnifique collection exposée par MM. Howard et fils dans le Palais du Champ-de-Mars. On sera heureux d'apprendre que cette collection, que plusieurs d'entre nous ont examiné avec un si vif intérêt, a obtenu une médaille d'or du jury international à l'Exposition universelle.

† Il y a des espèces botaniques de *Cinchona* dont le type peut avoir une écorce pauvre en alcaloïdes, lorsque, au contraire, quelqu'une de ses variétés peut en avoir une très-riche, et *vice versâ.* Le *C. lancifolia* et le *C. Calisaya* fournissent des exemples de ces anomalies.

‡ "La quinine a de préférence son siège dans le liber ou, pour parler plus exactement, dans le tissu cellulaire interposé aux fibres du liber, et que la cinchonine occupe plus particulièrement celui qui constitue la tunique ou enveloppe cellulaire proprement dite."—'Histoire Naturelle des Quinquinas,' p. 25.

Howard, one of the students of cinchonas best qualified to judge on chemical and pharmaceutical grounds, shares Weddell's conclusion, at all events so far that he does not consider the liber fibres, but the parenchyma, as the site of the alkaloids. I intend to explain Howard's views in another place, *as they almost entirely coincide with my own.*

Wigand asserts precisely the opposite view in his excellent 'Lehrbuch der Pharmakognosie,' page 112, "Alkaloid, that is to say quinine, has its seat within the liber, in the liber fibres." No other pharmaceutist expresses himself with so much decision on this subject, and he grounds his assertion on a course of acute and careful experiments.*

Wigand's assertion demands the greater consideration, since it is a repetition of Schacht's saying,† "I consider it probable that all alkaloids are products of the bast cells, and that quinine and chinchonine are only produced in the liber fibres of cinchonas."

With the first clause of this general assertion we have nothing to do; let us consider the second in its relation to cinchonas.

By experiments, which I need not repeat, Wigand discovered that the liber fabric had a power of absorbing and retaining the dye of cochineal in the same manner as a dyer's mordant. As it followed from his experiment that the liber fibres and not the parenchyma possessed this faculty, he concluded that the former must necessarily be the site of the alkaloid. I have, however, followed his experiments, and cannot say much for them. Wigand summarily rejects Weddell's argument, that the thickness of their cellular walls renders this quality impossible. He considers his own method rather intricate, and says it would be well, if possible, to find a simpler one.

He first found that the well-known reaction of Grähe became evident upon heating a cross-section of cinchona bark; and further, that it was possible so to divide pounded bark in a sieve as to obtain separately the parts richest in bast cells and the parenchyma. It was then evident that the latter was the poorest in alkaloid.‡ What follows will show that I must be allowed to doubt the validity of both these arguments in favour of Wigand's hypothesis.

I miss the microscopical proof that there had really been a division in the manner spoken of, and acknowledge that I was unable to accomplish it by the same means. In the common *C. Calisaya plana,* for instance, the parenchyma is usually entirely absent. Wigand's own confession,§ "If it were possible entirely to clear the parenchyma from the liber fibres, it would probably yield no alkaloid," shows that he himself was not fully satisfied with the result of the sieve experiment.

If, starting from the fact that the liber fibres are heavier than parenchyma, a piece of bark is taken, with rather long, numerous, and, if possible, isolated liber fibres, contained in tender parenchyma, a much more effectual separation will take place by washing.

I chose a variety of *C. Calisaya (Boliviana)* which is very brittle, smooth, and open, and which, in contradistinction to ordinary *C. Calisaya,* contains a good proportion of parenchyma and many laticiferous vessels. I touched small triturated portions of this bark with a little cold distilled water, rinsed away the loose parenchyma, rubbed the remainder again very gently, and treated it in the same way. Finally, after a little help with the pincers, I obtained liber fibres, which showed, when microscopically examined, only inconsiderable remnants of parenchyma, and were themselves uninjured.

The separated parenchyma was, however, less pure, it being almost impossible to clear it entirely from isolated liber fibres. The *C. Boliviana* thus dealt with yielded plentifully the red sublimate of Grähe's experiment, when heated in a glass tube, and a tolerable quantity of alkaloid came from the bark when touched with cold spirits of wine.

The separated liber fibres showed none of the reaction of Grähe, and even hot spirits of wine drew no alkaloid from them, whilst the parenchyma gave results in both respects similar to those of the unchanged bark. I made the same observations with *C. lancifolia.* It seems to me that this simple experiment proves, at least, that the woody liber fibres are not the sole or principal site of alkaloid, but far rather the parenchyma is so. There are, it seems to me, very few possible objections against this proof.

Wigand's assertion, that the liber fibres turned red when heated, is no doubt the result of his having worked with parenchyma as well, when the red sublimate from the latter might easily colour the liber fibres; but it may be said that Grähe's reaction is not a sufficiently delicate test to be of much account.

The question is not, however, to prove the absolute absence of alkaloid in the liber fibres, but much more its preponderance in the parenchyma. Nevertheless, I tried a few experiments which proved that in dried sago meal less than one per cent. of sulphate of quinine cannot be discovered by Grähe's reaction. The delicacy of the method, however, goes further with the bark itself, since it gives positive results if, for instance, *C. Boliviana* is mixed with five times the weight of sago. Since by Grähe's proof so alkaloid was to be found in the liber fibres, but was present in the parenchyma, can it be doubted that the latter yields the principal part of it. But the fact that spirits of wine drew no alkaloids from them deserves to count for much more. If alkaloid is contained in parenchyma, no one wishes to assert that the liber is wholly destitute of it. Even should this be the case in the living plant, it is highly probable that as the bark dries, small quantities may be absorbed by the liber fibres. In fact, my liber fibres, which seemed by ordinary treatment to contain no quinine, show slight traces of it by influorescence. Of how much account it is, however, to obtain slight traces of quinine in this optical way, can be imagined when it is remembered that the one-hundred-thousandth part of a milligram discovers itself in this manner. It is hardly necessary to remark that parenchyma, filtered with sulphuric acid, showed very evident fluorescence. A most serious fault might be found with the means of procuring my liber fibres, since of course cold water, even in the very smallest quantities, takes some alkaloid from the bark. The circumstance can only be thought of no consequence when it is remembered that I used it with great caution for a very short time. And at the same time it cannot be imagined that the liber fibres should thereby lose all their alkaloid and the parenchyma retain it. But even grant that an even amount of alkaloid is lost in the process by both structures, this does not in the least alter the conclusion *that the parenchyma contains the larger portion.*

* 'Botanische Zeitung,' vol. xx. pp. 137-143.   † Schacht, 'Anatomie und Physiologie der Gewächse,' Berlin, 1840, vol. i. p. 400.
‡ The opposite is shown by Howard's experiments on *China rubra dura.* Compare 'Nueva Quinologia,' Microse. Observ. fol. 5.
§ 'Botanische Zeitung,' vol. xx. p. 140.

D. (Page 29.)

Account of the State of the Cultivation of the Cinchona in Java in the Second Quarter of 1868. By C. VAN GORKOM.

During this quarter there were obtained about 10,666 plants of *C. Calisaya* (of which about 5000 were from Bolivian seeds), 13,845 *C. succirubra* (mostly from seeds from Ceylon), and 9840 *C. Condaminea*, so that at present the account of the plantations contains—

C. Calisaya	. . .	509,582
C. succirubra	. .	27,578
C. Condaminea	.	28,874
C. lancifolia	. .	573
C. micrantha	. .	386

Total 566,993 Plants.

Of these there are in the different establishments in connected gardens—

C. Calisaya	. .	330,809
C. succirubra	. .	5,003
C. Condaminea	. .	18,068
C. lancifolia	.	573
C. micrantha	.	343

Total 354,796

The state of the weather was less favourable for the youngest plantations; the continuous drought must also have half-checked the extension of the plantations. On the other hand, the preparation of the woodland was greatly promoted, and in two months sufficient land will be got ready for the following year. Free day-labourers were paid for 11,160 days' labour. The number of fully-engaged and more or less skilled workmen amounts to 120, of whom about one quarter are continuously employed in the nursery garden.

The development of the plantations of 1866 and 1867 is very satisfactory. On the Tilu and Tankuban-Prahu Mountains it may be called unusually good; on the Malawar Mountains the gardens are rather behindhand. Without any particular reason being manifest, the leaves of the C. Calisaya pucker and dry up, and their power of life appears to slumber. In other establishments this has only exceptionally been the case. In 1866 a similar sickness showed itself in the former year's plantation; nevertheless the consequences were not serious, and this plantation has so far extended itself since, that in the year 1871 some thousand kilogrammes of bark may be expected to be gathered therefrom, in order to bring these first proofs of the Java cultivation to market. It is to be hoped that some seasonable showers will bring the Malawar plantation again into its normal state.

Many *C. Condaminea* plants already begin to blossom, and from single *C. lancifolia* plants we may expect fruit towards the end of this year. Seeds of the *C. Calisaya* were continuously gathered in still larger quantity, even under the plants which were produced in 1865 from American seeds. Some plants of the *C. Calisaya vera* are loaded with ripe fruit. Through the friendly and efficacious assistance of Dr. Thwaites, of Paradenia (Ceylon), the stock of *C. succirubra* and *C. Condaminea* plants was largely increased. This help is very highly prized, and its continuance will be very welcome in future. The *C. Calisaya* seeds received from Bolivia have relatively produced bad results, for only 5000 seedlings were produced therefrom.

Most of the raising-houses have required considerable repairs: two new contrivances were completed, and measures taken that the kinds of *Cinchona* which have not produced any seeds in Java should afford young plants with greater quickness.

First, in September and October great numbers of seeds of the *C. Calisaya* will be sown, since further steps must be taken to protect the plantations against ruin in a rainy season, in order to have from nine to twelve months after the sowing of the seed, the plants strong enough to plant out in the open ground.

Seeds of the Cinchona have been continuously desired by private individuals, but no results have yet shown a happy treatment. If people would trust with confidence in the cost of the transport, these attempts would certainly succeed better, and the universal sympathy for private plantations would be in consequence aroused and increased.

Mr. Van Gorkom says, in reference to the Calisaya:—"Dr. Scheffer has confirmed my supposition that the seeds ripened in Java of the plants raised by Junghuhn (5000 plants) are not Calisaya; indeed, this sort of Cinchona appears, like the *Pahudiana*, to be a sort hitherto unknown. It is not described by Weddell. Miquel is closely examining it. These trees grow splendidly, and contain the double quantity of alkaloids (0·7 = 1·3 per cent.) compared with the *Pahudiana*. Would the trade purchase well such a bark? Should this question be answered in the affirmative, I could easily bring 10,000 pounds into the market, for I have caused the plantations of this sort in the year 1864 to be lightened, and have constantly kept the eye upon them, so that the beautiful high and strong trees should remain. The greater part of these are eight years old, and hundreds of these are to be found which could give three to five pounds of bark, whilst I will take as a mean produce only two pounds."

(Obligingly sent by Dr. Hasskarl.)

L

E. (Page 29.)

Report of an Analysis of the Eighth Remittance of Bark from India. By J. E. Howard, F.L.S.

TO THE UNDER-SECRETARY OF STATE FOR INDIA.

September 1st, 1868.

Sir,—I have to report on specimens of bark collected in March of the present year, and sent to me for analysis, as follows :—

No. 1, *C. succirubra*, being "the third harvest of renewed bark," is most interesting, as it showed more completely than any sent hitherto the aspect of the red bark from South America, and has in all respects a superior appearance. In examining it chemically, I found that it presented also more exactly the counterpart of that composition which I have described as being commonly observed in the analysis of the older bark of this species. I hoped to obtain a larger produce than last time, but was disappointed in finding a smaller amount of salts of quinine, viz. 6·15 per cent., against 8·45 per cent. in the specimen of renewed bark from the same tree on which I had the honour to report in February, 1867.

The above figures give the *relative* commercial value of the two specimens; but, as I thought it desirable to obtain all the information in my power, I endeavoured, in two experiments, with a sufficient quantity of bark (¼ lb.) in each, to arrive at the most correct results. From the first I obtained quinine as alkaloid, capable of being formed into, and equivalent to 5·33 per cent. of sulphate of quinine. From the second, by a process somewhat varied, I obtained in crystallizations of refined oxalate 4·80 per cent., and remaining in the liquor as more soluble (in part, perhaps, oxalate of cinchonidine) 0·60, together 5·40 per cent. oxalate of quinine. In both cases there was an inevitable loss through the product being more exactly purified; and, therefore, this must be borne in mind in comparing these figures with those previously given; but, even at this lowest or *minimum* scale of production, the results are really surprisingly good, though not equal to the hopes entertained by Mr. M'Ivor.

The explanation of a smaller produce *of sulphate of quinine* appears to me to be found in the *idiosyncrasy* of this particular species, which I have described to the best of my power in my 'Illustrations of the Nueva Quinologia,' *sub voce C. succirubra*.

I am pleased to find that Mr. Broughton, in his First Report, corroborates what I have said as to the difficulty of obtaining the alkaloids in a pure state from this species, a difficulty which increases with the age of the tree. On this account, I must again urge the necessity of carefully ascertaining what species are likely to yield the best *permanent* results.

The precipitated hydrated alkaloids, in a subsequent examination of a small portion of the present bark against a re-examination of a portion remaining from the second harvest, gave me for the *second harvest* of renewed bark,—

Alkaloids dried at the temperature of the air	.	10·60
Of which soluble in ether, quinine, etc.	8·70 ⎫	
„ „ insoluble in ether, cinchonine, etc.	1·90 ⎭	

For the *third or present harvest* of renewed bark,—

Alkaloids dried at the temperature of the air	.	11·20
Of which soluble in ether, quinine, etc.	9·40 ⎫	
„ „ insoluble in ether, cinchonine, etc.	1·80 ⎭	

It will be seen that the proportion of alkaloid has increased, but this would be no guide to the commercial value, which is almost entirely regulated by the proportion capable of being converted into crystallized salts. More valuable commercial information, consequently, will be gained from the following corrected analysis :—

Quinine (as sulphate)	.	5·33
„ uncrystallizable	.	2·00 (?)
		——
		7·33
Cinchonidine	.	1·14
Cinchonicine	.	0·58
		——
		9·00

I have attached a (?) to the weight of the proportion of uncrystallizable quinine, which it was impossible to ascertain exactly from so small a quantity of bark. Moreover, from its great implication with resinous colouring matter, I am led to doubt the possibility of obtaining any part of it as crystallized sulphate of quinine on a large scale. This uncrystallizable portion is, therefore, unimportant, and not to be reckoned, from a commercial point of view, as possessing any value to the purchaser of such bark for manufacturing purposes.*

The analysis of No. 2, "Root bark from a tree of *C. succirubra* seven years old," presented much interest, as bearing on the question as to which of several modes of cultivation is to be preferred, since it has recently been proposed to cultivate the plant, like madder, solely for the roots.

I consequently have forwarded about half the sample of No. 2, and also No. 3 (of which a very small quantity was sent from India) to Dr. de Vrij, as it was desirable thus to arrive at a consentaneous agreement on the value of the root bark, which I have always regarded unfavourably, judging from the root bark of the *C. Calisaya, var. Josephiana*, occasionally found in the market.

---

* The weight of the crystallisable, and consequently more valuable, portion, was ascertained by the following process:—The 6·15 per cent. (as above) having been precipitated, the precipitate was dissolved in ether, separating thus the cinchonidine and the quinine, then dried at 212° F. It must be understood that quinine thus obtained from the *C. succirubra*, although sufficiently pure to pass the tests required in commerce, retains some cinchonidine, which can be separated by solution in acid and subsequent treatment with iodide of potassium.

The analysis was troublesome, although the hydrated alkaloids were obtained in a state more free than often from colouring matter. The weight of the precipitated alkaloids appeared to be 12·75 per cent., but this hopeful amount did not yield proportionate results, probably from an amount of wax and resin being carried down with the alkaloids. I obtained with difficulty a small crystallization of sulphate of quinine, and the remaining liquor, when precipitated, dissolved in ether, and the solution left to concentrate by evaporation, furnished crystals of cinchonidine adhering to the sides of the vessel, and at last uncrystallizable quinine containing a portion of quinidine.

The remarkable feature was the large production of fine cinchonine, almost insoluble in ether, yielding good crystals from spirit of wine, and these, when formed into sulphate, giving the very characteristic salt. In all this, the root bark is decidedly superior; but, it will be observed, it is *cinchonine*, and not *quinine*, that (at all events in this species) is the product of this root bark. I give the total as follows :—

Quinine (as sulphate) . . 1·75		
„ uncrystallisable . . 4·50 (?)		
—— 6·25		
Cinchonine . . . . . 3·00		
Cinchonicine, water, and gum resin . . 3·50		
12·75		

This root bark would not be of more value than that mentioned above (of the *C. Josephiana*), unless it were wanted for the extraction of cinchonine.

No. 3. I shall transmit the report of the analysis when I receive it from Dr. de Vrij.

No. 4 consists of four pieces of fine-looking crown bark, apparently not intended for chemical analysis.

Nos. 5, 6, and 7 are interesting to me, and will, I hope, furnish some facts for a work which I am publishing, "On the Quinology of the East Indian Plantations." They appear to be intended rather for microscopical examination than for chemical analysis. The seeds of No. 7 have been sent to Kew.

I beg to remain, yours very truly,

JOHN ELIOT HOWARD.

SUPPLEMENT.

Copy of a Letter from Dr. DE VRIJ *to* J. E. HOWARD, Esq., *containing Analysis of No.* 2 *Root Bark.*

The Hague, August 30th, 1868.

The sample of No. 2 *Cinchona succirubra, root bark, from a tree seven years old,* with your letter of the 21st instant, duly reached me, and immediately I set at work to analyse this bark, which was very welcome to me, particularly because now you have the opportunity to judge by yourself of the richness of the *root bark*, at least, of the cultivated cinchonas.

I found in the bark 11¾ per cent. of alkaloids, and 0·467 per cent of cinchona bitter (kinovic acid). The part of the alkaloids soluble in ether amounts to 4·31 per cent. of the bark. Although these 4·31 per cent. are soluble in ether, they do not entirely consist of quinine (crystallisable), but contain another alkaloid also soluble in ether. As you expressed your wish to obtain the results of my experiments within about ten days, I have not been able to ascertain with certainty which is this alkaloid which accompanies the crystallizable quinine in its etherial solution. I suspect it is the amorphous alkaloid which I always find in the Indian barks, but am not yet quite sure of it. I obtained beautiful herapathite from the part of the alkaloids dissolved by ether, so that there is no doubt that this root bark contains really crystallizable quinine. In treating the total amount of alkaloid with ether, I had some reason to expect to obtain also cinchonidine. In this I was, however, frustrated, for I could not find till now with certainty its presence. All this moment that I write this letter my result is that the mentioned bark is rich in alkaloids, of which the part *insoluble* in ether consists chiefly of *cinchonine*. If cinchonidine is perhaps also present, it can only be a very small quantity, not to be compared with the large quantity which I obtained from the stem bark of *C. succirubra*.

Copy of a Letter from Dr. DE VRIJ *to* J. E. HOWARD, Esq., *containing Analysis of No.* 3 *Root Bark.*

September 18th, 1868.

Together with your valued letter of September 3rd, I received the No. 3 of root bark from *C. succirubra.* . . . As the amount of the powdered bark dried at 212° F. was only 19·5 grammes, I divided this quantity into two parts, viz., one of 10 grammes (the quantity which I always use), and one of the remaining 9·5 grammes. From the first I obtained 1·202 grammes, and from the second 1·088 grammes of alkaloids. The average percentage of alkaloids in *this* red bark is therefore 11·748 per cent., whilst the amount of kinovic acid is 0·676 per cent. The combined amount of the obtained alkaloids, viz. 2·29 grammes, was dissolved in dilute acetic acid, by which treatment only an impounderable trace of dark brown resinous matter remained undissolved. As the acetic solution proved to contain no quinidine, it was shaken with caustic soda and ether. The following day the etherial solution, which was lemon-coloured, was evaporated, and the residue dried at 212° F. Its amount was 0·931 gramme; this root bark contains, therefore, 4·774 per cent. of alkaloid soluble in ether. I obtained from these 0·931 gramme beautiful herapathite, but found, in the meantime, that the largest part of this alkaloid soluble in ether is *not* quinine, but an amorphous alkaloid. I am still occupied with researches to find out the real nature of this amorphous alkaloid. . . . The remaining alkaloids, which were not dissolved by ether, proved to be *cinchouine*, with only a trace of cinchonidine. In this root, as in the former, I found the cinchonine particularly fit to crystallize, and consequently I obtained beautiful sulphate of cinchonine from it.

J. E. HOWARD, Esq., *to* C. R. MARKHAM, Esq.

For the guidance of the Indian Government, I send the foregoing interesting and well-executed analysis, and add that it accords most nearly with the previous analyses by Dr. de Vrij and myself of No. 2 *Root Bark* of larger size, but of the same parcel, and that these specimens of root bark would command but a low price in the London market, from the causes before tated. I do not think the root bark of *this species* would repay cultivation.

ADDENDA ET CORRIGENDA.

MR. BROUGHTON'S REPORT, AUGUST, 1868.

Since the foregoing sheets were sent to press, I have received from Mr. Broughton a copy of his latest Report,* dated 17th August, 1868.

I am pleased to find that the contents of this letter tend greatly to the confirmation of the views I have advanced, especially in the following particulars :—

1. In reference to the value of the *C. succirubra* as a species for cultivation, which I have always thought over-estimated (and never more so than in recent accounts from Jamaica), Mr. Broughton says :—

"My experience of the Red Bark plantations does not lead to the conclusion that the amount of Quinine has shared in the increase observable in that of the other alkaloids. To this subject I shall subsequently return."

"Bark of *C. succirubra*, grown in the Wynaad at an elevation probably not exceeding 2400 feet, was *thinner* than that of Neilgherry growth, and that of good appearance gave but 0·5 per cent. of Sulphate of Quinine, and 2·9 of Sulphate of Cinchonidine, showing that Quinine is formed in much less quantities at low elevations." The whole of Mr. Broughton's experience leads to the conclusion that "a high mean temperature is *adverse to the yield of Quinine*, but NOT *to that of Cinchonidine*."

"The bark of two trees, after a sample had been analysed, was covered in one tree with a shield of tinned plate, and in the other with black cloth. The object was to keep the bark in darkness, while access of air was not impeded. The result of subsequent analyses were as follows :—

	Tree covered with tinned plate.		Tree covered with black cloth.		
	Original bark.	Bark after ten months' protection.	Original bark.	Bark after six months' protection.	Bark after ten months' protection.
Total alkaloids . . .	5·29	8·10	5·04	6·91	7·92
Quinine	2·16	1·65	2·26	2·03	2·34
Cinchonidine and Cinchonine	3·13	6·45	2·78	4·88	5·58

"The foregoing experiments agree in showing that deprivation of sunshine has had the effect of increasing the amount of alkaloid in the bark. The alkaloid was obtained crystallised with nearly the same readiness as in mossed bark. The amount of Quinine has *not*, however, been increased, as in the case of mossing. This is a circumstance which I did not expect, and it is opposed to deductions from other experiments. It is, however, a fact, and will doubtless be explained by increased knowledge of the subject."

The trees covered with black cloth or with tinned plate, in this experiment, would not thereby be shielded from the heating effect of the sun's rays, and probably on this account coincide in their product of *Cinchonidine* with those which I have described as grown in sunshine.

"It is a fact that, in the Chinchona barks of South India (considered as a whole), the replacement of Quinine by Chinchonidine obtains to a greater proportion of the total yield of alkaloids than in those of South America. The actual amount of the substitution varies greatly in single trees, both according to its variety and the conditions to which it is exposed. The practical effect of this peculiarity is compensated for by the large total yield of the alkaloids. For medicinal purposes, it appears, from the recent medical trials, that it is of little importance which of the two alkaloids are produced. Nevertheless, the causes which produce the replacement are obviously of the greatest interest in connection with Chinchona cultivation. There must be several proximate causes, and it will, I think, be evident from the foregoing experimental results, that they are in progress of being elicited. Thus it appears that *a low mean temperature within certain limits is favourable to the production of Quinine,*† as is also

* Proceedings of the Madras Government Revenue Department, September 22, 1868, No. 384. Read the following letter from J. Broughton, Esq., Quinologist to Government.

† The italics are mine, to direct special attention to these important observations.—J. E. H.

the loose cellular structure of the bark produced by artificial means. To these must be added a circumstance that I have long observed, more especially among the varieties of *C. officinalis*, that trees which are from their position fully exposed to sunshine have a proportionally larger amount of Chinchonidine than those grown in shade.

"Mr. Howard, to whom I communicated this observation, informed me that it quite agrees with his experience. The yield of Quinine in the Ceylon Crown barks was greater in those grown in shade than in those fully exposed. Dr. De Vrij has observed the same peculiarity.

"The same fact harmonizes with the opinion prevailing in South America, that the bark of Uritusinga varies in quality according to the aspect of its situation with respect to the sun. If it be the *heat* of the sunshine that produces these effects, it will be seen that exposed bark would in many respects be under the same conditions as that grown in a warmer climate. The sunshine, which is powerless to warm the dry and diathermanous air of the Neilgherries, falling on the bark, at once raises its temperature.

"These observations derive additional force from the consideration, that it is in this respect of effective heat-giving sunshine that the climate of the mountain ranges of South India differs from that of the Chinchona regions of South America. With the same annual mean atmospheric temperature, the climate of the Neilgherries differs from that of the bark regions, in having six months of unclouded sunshine when the singular dryness of the atmosphere robs the rays of none of their heating power. The bark countries of the Andes are, unlike ours, situated in a region of perpetual trade-winds, which, as our monsoons, bring their abundant rains and fogs during the greater part of the year to interrupt the sunshine. The travels of Markham, Karsten, Spruce, Boussingault, and many others bear full testimony to this."

The elevation of 6000 to 7000 feet appears to be most favourable to the yield of Quinine in the *C. succirubra;* above the latter height it diminishes.

"The fifth year of the life of the Red Bark trees is marked by a great increase in the number of the liber fibres of the bark, by which that portion becomes thoroughly developed. There appear to be some grounds for the conclusion that this development is not favourable to the yield of Quinine."

"Frequent analyses made of the Red Barks during the last eighteen months have clearly shown that the yield of alkaloids varies according to the season of the year. The ratio that the amount of Quinine bears to the other alkaloids appears also to vary. Periodic analyses were begun fourteen months since, for the purpose of ascertaining the times of maximum and minimum yield, but at least a year more must elapse before I obtain sufficient data to decide this important subject. I may, however, state that the point of maximum yield falls within the period comprised between the beginning of February and the end of May."

I have remarked on the great variability which I have found in the products of the *C. succirubra* from South America, which may partly depend on the above cause. If I were forming a plantation, I should certainly not depend on this species as my mainstay.

2. Mr. Broughton agrees with me in a favourable estimate of the Crown Barks, from which, however, must be deducted the disadvantage of a slower growth, and a consequent—perhaps one-third—less formation of bark than in the *C. succirubra.* The largest yield of Quinine in these barks occurred at the height of 8000 feet.

"The trees planted at the lowest slopes of the latter, yield barks which are also inferior in other respects, since they contain *resinous* and *colouring* matters which increase the labour of purifying the alkaloids. *The cortical fibres are also more numerous in the low-grown Crown Barks.* I have also detected Quinidine in these barks. The Quinine is in great part replaced by Cinchonidine, *exactly as in low-grown Red Barks.*"

"I have already expressed my conviction of the great value of our Crown Barks. Further investigation has given no reason to alter that opinion. The Quinine which they contain yields a pure white crystalline sulphate with ease. Many specimens I have met with have been actually free from "uncrystallizable Quinine." Hence the Quinine is frequently so pure as to yield its theoretical amount of crystallized sulphate. I have met with specimens of Crown Bark which yield upwards of five per cent. of purified alkaloid.

"Mr. Howard (whose correspondence and assistance have been of great service to my work) has informed me that he has satisfactorily identified a sub-variety of our *Chinchona officinalis* with that which yielded the bark known as *Amarilla del Rey.* This is a sort which has long enjoyed a high reputation among Pharmaceutists and Quinine manufacturers, and its possession is a very fortunate circumstance. It appears very easy to work, and yields Quinine readily, crystallizable as sulphate. In actual amount, however, it does not appear to differ essentially from its companion sub-varieties.

"Among the Crown Barks which were grown from seeds brought by Mr. Cross, are a few scattered trees, which present a marked difference from the rest of their companions. The leaves are of a narrow lanceolate shape. My attention being directed to the study of those varieties whose numerical importance claimed the earliest observation, it was not till recently that I made an analysis of this variety. Surprised by the result, I took the precaution of making an analysis of the adjoining trees of *Chinchona officinalis*, in order to eliminate the possible influence of peculiar conditions of soil, site, etc.

"The percentages of the respective alkaloids stand thus :—

	Bark of Lanceolate species.	Bark of adjoining trees.
Total alkaloids	8·0	4·48
Quinine	7·15	2·06
Chinchonidine and Chinchonine . .	0·85	2·42
Sulphate of Quinine obtained crystallized . .	7·37	Undetermined.
Do. Chinchonidine obtained crystallized .	0·15	Do.

"The specimen, therefore, was of the finest bark in our possession. I do not think I over-state, when I add that, in yield of Quinine, it is of the finest quality that has ever been recorded. It possesses every characteristic constituting excellence. It yields alkaloids in such purity that the first crystallization gives sulphate of Quinine, which stands the usual tests as well as the refined salt. I would earnestly recommend that the plant be extensively propagated, and as rapidly as possible. The possession of this species is a most fortunate circumstance."*

I have also had the honour to present the Government with young plants from a small tree in my possession, with which Mr. M'Ivor was so much pleased, that he took out a layer which he himself had made of it. I name this provisionally *C. Forbesiana*, to commemorate Mr. David Forbes, who, after many adventures (which I have described in a paper sent to the Botanical Congress in 1866, page 199), brought the seed to England. I may possibly describe both these kinds more particularly in a future part. For the present, I will only add that the analogy of the leaf of the *C. Forbesiana* is with the *C. lancifolia*, but that of the flowers, which have unfortunately not advanced with me beyond the state of buds, seems to be with *C. micrantha*.

3. In reference to mossing the bark, and the reproduction of the bark after it has been removed from the trees, Mr. Broughton has the following remarks confirmatory of the views expressed by myself:—

"The bark of trees that have been subjected to the mossing treatment introduced by Mr. M'Ivor has been so abundantly examined by Mr. Howard, from specimens supplied at intervals for that purpose, that repetition by myself of the experiments on the same limited scale appears almost supererogatory. The following analyses may be adduced as quite corroborating former ones :—

	No. 1. Bark of C. succirubra sixteen months under moss.	No. 2. Bark of same trees renewed under moss sixteen months.
Total alkaloids . . .	10·72	8·22
Quinine	4·31	5·14
Chinchonine and Chinchonidine . .	6·41	3·08
Total sulphates obtained crystallized . .	9·27	4·67
Sulphate of Quinine	4·02	3·87
Do. Chinchonidine . . .	5·25	0·80

" The barks yield by mossing a greatly increased amount of alkaloid, and in a state which permits them to crystallize with facility as sulphates. The bark No. 2, renewed under moss, was thinner than natural bark, and *lost more weight on drying*. It should be remembered, however, that the renewed bark was sixteen, while the natural bark was sixty-six months old. This specimen was remarkable for the large amount of Chinchoniæ it contained. Had the sulphate of this base been reckoned among the total sulphates, their amount would have been upwards of six per cent. As already remarked by Mr. Howard, freshly-renewed bark contains a considerable amount of uncrystallizable Quinine.† I have continually observed this peculiarity of young bark, whether it be obtained from young trees directly, or produced by "renewal" on older trees. It would seem that it is as uncrystallizable Quinine that the alkaloids are first formed by the natural processes in the plant. Thus, from the 3·23 per cent. of Quinine found in some young Red Bark two and a half years old, but 1·97 of Sulphate of Quinine was obtainable crystallized ; while in some bark sixteen months old, but one-fifth of the Quinine found would give a crystalline sulphate.‡

" The process of mossing the bark appears to require trial on a scale in which the increase, both of bark and alkaloid, could be systematically determined, and the *cost*, compared with other methods of cropping the bark, such as coppicing, etc. These points are obviously necessary to an estimation of the practical value of the method, and at present are only guessed at. The repeated treatment of single trees, and analyses of the bark after so many concurrent experiments, seems comparatively useless labour, while there exist so many other questions of a chemical nature to be settled. Unless, therefore, Government are pleased to direct otherwise, I shall only give the subject that attention which its actual practical working demands, or that its connection with the histological chemistry of the plant may require."

4. I have mentioned that Mr. Broughton agrees with me that the liber fibres are not the seat of the alkaloids. Mr. Broughton adds, to a paragraph already quoted, the following information :—

"The opinion of authorities as to the principal seat of Quinine in the bark has been divided. Weddell, Wigand, Schleiden, and others have concluded, on theoretical grounds, that the liber is the part of the bark in which the alkaloids are situated ; Howard, on the contrary, by direct trial, has satisfied himself that the main seat of the alkaloids is in the cellular portions of the bark which are external to the liber. Having far greater facilities for determining this question than any other chemist has

* Mr. Broughton suggests that "it is not improbable that the species may be the *C. Pitayensis*, whose excellence it possesses." Mr. Batcock has brought home a large collection of specimens of Chinchonæ, and among them this important species appears represented by leafy branches of foliage, resembling the *C. lancifolia* of Dr. Karsten, but that rather in the general habit of the plant than in the exact shape of the leaf. It is certainly *not* the *C. Pitayensis* as represented in a specimen brought by Cross, and in my possession, of the *Quina roja* of the Piñon of Pitayo, but may *probably* belong to one of the forms of *Chinchona lancifolia* in the region of Popayan ; that called the *Culisaya of Santa Fé* is very rich in Quinine in its native habitat at the head of the valleys of the Cauca and Magdalena.
† But see the microscopical observations for my views on this point.—J. E. H.
‡ In these young barks the injurious resin abounds.—J. E. H.

hitherto possessed, I repeated the experiment that Mr. Howard had made, using, instead of the dried South American bark, the bark of *C. succirubra*, fresh from the tree. The liber was separated from the external cellular portion, and the two portions were then submitted to analysis. The analyses were made at a season favourable to the yield of alkaloids.

	First series.		Second series.	
	Liber.	Cellular portion.	Liber.	Cellular portion.
Total alkaloids . . .	5·94	7·98	6·85	8·00
Quinine	0·7	2·25	0·85	3·25
Chinchonidine and Chincho-				
nine	5·24	5·74	6·00	4·75
Sulphate of Quinine . .	Undetermined.	Undetermined.	0·9	2·8
Do. Chinchonidine .	Do.	Do.	4·1	4·2

A similar experiment was made with bark five and a half years old that had been under moss for seventeen months.

	Liber.	Cellular portion.
Total alkaloids .	9·80	11·83
Quinine	2·89	5·49
Chinchonidine and Chinchonine . .	6·91	6·34
Crystallized Sulphate of Quinine obtained . . .	2·44	5·1
Do. do. Chinchonidine obtained . .	4·74	4·84

" The whole of the above trials corroborate those of Mr. Howard, in showing that the external cellular part of the bark is markedly the richest in Quinine, and, to a less extent, richer in total alkaloids. When the bark becomes older, and the liber more woody, it is probable that these qualities will be still more apparent. It is remarkable that mossing, which increases the yield of Quinine, also has a tendency to thicken the cellular or less organized portion of the bark. The freshly-renewed barks, which, as shown above, contain principally Quinine, consist nearly entirely of cellular tissue. Hence, existing evidence is adverse to allowing the bark to obtain an age when liber would be formed at a greater rate than the cellular tissues of the bark."

5. Mr. Broughton's account of the green colouring-matter of the leaves agrees with those presented by myself to the reader. The lamented death of Dr. Herapath prevents the possibility of the completion of his researches, but I am inclined to believe that Mr. Broughton's observations, when finished, will coincide with those recorded by Dr. Herapath with his usual accuracy, copies of which he sent me in letters now in my possession.

6. Mr. Broughton agrees with preceding chemists, in looking upon the formation of the alkaloids as depending upon ammonia, and has the following good practical suggestion :—

" Ammonia has been present in every specimen of Indian bark that I have examined. The hypothesis has been propounded that this substance, which is itself really an alkaloid, is a step in the formation of Quinine, etc., and is, so to speak, the frame-work of their constitution. The idea of an essential connection between ammonia and the vegetable alkaloids dates from the early part of the century, and advance of knowledge has but increased its probability. As far as I am aware, the action of ammoniacal manures (so largely employed in European agriculture) has never been systematically studied, when applied to the alkaloid-producing plants, although the idea of supplying the elements required in the elaboration of these peculiar products is a plausible one. I would suggest that small plots of the two leading varieties of Cinchona in our possession be each manured with guano in one case, and in the other with common sulphate of ammonia, such as is sold in Europe for agricultural purposes, commencing when the plants are a year old. This is an experiment in cultivation that must be tried sooner or later, since the question of the action of manures is one that obviously suggests itself. The chemical study of the effect, even if it be a negative one, will be of great interest."

7. Mr. Broughton was the first to ascertain, and to publish (paragraph 20) the existence of alkaloid in the heart-wood of *C. succirubra*. His amount, 0·08 to 0·11 per cent., agrees well with mine.

UEBER DIE CHINAKULTUR AUF JAVA.

I HAVE received, under this head, the German translation of a paper in the Dutch periodical 'Gids,' of May, 1868, in which the writer gives his account of the progress of the cultivation of the Cinchonæ in Java. The Dutch have the honour of leading the way in this useful enterprise, and therefore it is the more to be regretted that the mistakes, which were certain to be incurred in a new undertaking, should have been rendered more disastrous by the party spirit with which the whole subject appears to have been agitated, even in the Legislature.

It is extremely unpleasant to come in contact with such a state of things, and I find that I am censured for not being sufficiently one-sided in the dispute. The writer in 'Gids' says "Mr. Howard, who described the unfortunate sort as a new species in his noble work on the Cinchonæ, although he at first, with reason, brought its usefulness into question, afterwards took a position of weakness and uncertainty as the conflict began to wax warm," etc.

To this I have only to reply that I have published such information as came to my hands as correctly as I could, and intend still to do so. I see no occasion to alter my account of the species given in the 'Nueva Quinologia,' and still believe that it is without value if looked at simply as a source for the extraction of Quinine; but as regards the *root-bark*, I have, personally, no information to oppose to the favourable estimate elsewhere entertained, and must therefore maintain a position of "uncertainty" till this is removed by those who can decide the question. If the *C. Pahudiana* be looked upon in another point of view, viz. as a possible source of bark for pharmaceutical purposes, I have shown in my reports, given to the Government of British India, on specimens from Ootacamund, that the quill bark is not only *not* worthless, but that such quills as those sent by McIvor were actually preferred to other kinds sent with them by dealers most competent to judge in London; and this not without reason, from their taste, appearance, and chemical composition. I cannot, therefore, agree with those who recommended the superfluous labour of cutting down the trees; neither can I rank this plant "among the best sorts of all," as, it seems, some have attempted to do. The trees, having now many years' growth, might, perhaps, furnish quill bark fit for the home market; and I shall be surprised if it is not at least equally valued there with the bark of the so-called *C. Calisaya*, which, I am afraid, will prove "unfortunate" also; at least if it produces but 1·8 per cent., as described by Van Gorkom.

I have now specimens of the *C. Pahudiana* in healthy growth, and am confirmed in my view of its being a new species, "quite distinct," as Dr. Woddell avers, from the *C. Carabayensis*.

Dr. de Vrij remarks:*—

"Tandis que le gouvernement néerlandais, éclairé par ses savants conseillers (voyez 'De Gids,' mai 1868), considérait comme superflue la présence d'un chimiste, chargé spécialement d'éclairer sans discontinuité de ses lumières et de ses expériences la marche de la culture des cinchonas et faisait détruire (ce qui a été exécuté par les ordres du gouverneur général Hœt Van de Boele à la fin de 1863) le laboratoire de chimie qui avait été érigé à grands frais à proximité des plantations de cinchonas, le gouvernement anglais a été précisément d'une opinion tout opposée et a envoyé dans ce but en 1866 M. Broughton à Ootacamund. La représentation nationale des Pays-Bas paraît toutefois partager l'opinion du gouvernement anglais : cela résulte de ce fait que la deuxième chambre des États-Généraux a donné le 14 juillet 1865 son approbation au rapport de la commission choisie dans son sein pour examiner les pièces produites par le ministre des colonies relativement à la culture des cinchonas à Java : or ce rapport se termine de la manière suivante.

"'Pour atteindre le résultat désiré, il sera du reste nécessaire d'étudier sans discontinuité dans des conditions diverses avec tous les moyens fournis par la science les différentes sortes de cinchona poussant actuellement à Java, afin de pouvoir ainsi arriver à connaître dans quelles circonstances il se forme dans l'écorce une quantité de quinine aussi grande que possible.'

"Il est fâcheux que le gouvernement n'ait paru tenir aucun compte de ce désir et que nous soyons par suite encore actuellement fort peu édifiés sur les conditions dans lesquelles a lieu dans les différentes espèces de cinchona la formation de la plus grande quantité possible de quinine."

I have only to add, in justice to Dr. Vrij, that it did not occur to me, whilst referring in page 6, to the solicitude with which I conducted the first experiment on bark of *C. succirubra* from Ootacamund, to state that Dr. de Vrij had *previously* obtained and described alkaloids from the plantations in Java. (See the 'Répertoire de Chimie,' October, 1860, p. 315.)

M. HARDY, SUR LA CULTURE DU QUINQUINA EN ALGÉRIE.

THE above pamphlet has been sent me by M. le Dr. J. L. Soubeiran. It is valuable to all who have any intention of commencing Cinchona plantations in any extra-tropical region. It has confirmed me in a fear, which the experience of the past summer of 1868 has induced in my mind, that I have spoken rather too sanguinely in the early portion of this work of the possibility of any member of the family becoming at all acclimatized in our regions. The heat and drought of summer and the frosts of winter seem almost alike inimical to the success of the enterprise.

CULTIVATION OF CINCHONA IN TEXAS.

DR. THOMAS ANTISELL appears to have prepared a memoir on this subject, which forms part of the Commission of Agriculture for 1866. Seeds of the *C. succirubra* and *Condaminea* were procured by the United States Minister residing in Ecuador. The latter only germinated in 1864, in the experimental garden of the Department of Agriculture at Washington, but owing to unfavourable circumstances the plants were but weakly, and it was intended to transport them to more propitious regions.

It had been supposed that Texas might present favourable localities, but these, according to Dr. Antisell are more likely to be found towards the frontiers of Mexico, below the zone of the *Sequoia*. ('Journal de Pharmacie et de Chimie,' Jan. 1869.)

ERRATUM.

Page 11, line 29. "By" *should be* "of."

---

* 'Journal de Pharmacie et de Chimie,' Jan. 1869, p. 24.

M

www.ingramcontent.com/pod-product-compliance
Lightning Source LLC
Chambersburg PA
CBHW021542270326
41930CB00008B/1334